99 Astonishing Cities and Civilizations
Found in the Bible

museum of the Bible

BOOKS

99 Astonishing Cities and Civilizations Found in the Bible
© 2017 Museum of the Bible, Inc., Washington, DC 20014
Published by Worthy Publishing Group, a division of Worthy Media, Inc. in association with Museum of the Bible.

ISBN-10: 1945470038
ISBN-13: 978-1945470035

Library of Congress number for 99 Cities: 2017947426

Unless otherwise indicated, Scripture quotations are from the ESV® Bible (The Holy Bible, English Standard Version®), copyright © 2001 by Crossway, a publishing ministry of Good News Publishers. Used by permission. All rights reserved.

Scripture quotation marked NRSV is taken from the New Revised Standard Version Bible, copyright © 1989 the Division of Christian Education of the National Council of the Churches of Christ in the United States of America. Used by permission. All rights reserved.

Scripture quotations marked NIV are taken from the Holy Bible, New International Version®, NIV® Copyright ©1973, 1978, 1984, 2011 by Biblica, Inc.® Used by permission. All rights reserved worldwide.

Scripture quotations marked NLT are taken from the Holy Bible, New Living Translation, copyright ©1996, 2004, 2007, 2013, 2015 by Tyndale House Foundation. Used by permission of Tyndale House Publishers, Inc., Carol Stream, Illinois 60188. All rights reserved.

Produced with the assistance of Hudson Bible.

Printed in the USA

1 2 3 4 5 6 7 8 9 LAKE 22 21 20 19 18 17

Cover image: iStock
Everett Collection: 10
Getty Images: 79
Deposit Photos: 31, 32, 33
Lightstock: 85, 96
The Bible People: 15, 21, 36, 21, 74, 93, 97, 98
Istockphoto: 19, 53, 54, 58, 60, 61, 63, 66, 69, 75
Bible Places:
   © A.D. Riddle/BiblePlaces.com: 11, 14, 17, 46, 51, 52, 56, 65
   © William Schlegel/BiblePlaces.com: 40, 47, 79
   © Library of Congress/Lifeintheholyland.com/Bible Places: 20, 78
   © Todd Bolen/BiblePlaces.com: 9, 21, 25, 27, 44, 46, 50, 64, 69, 76, 77, 80, 81, 82, 84, 87, 94
Shutterstock: 6, 8, 11, 12, 15, 18, 21, 22, 23, 24, 25, 26, 28, 30, 31, 34, 37, 38, 39, 41, 42, 45, 48, 51, 55, 57, 68, 71, 72, 74, 76, 78, 82, 83, 85, 86, 88, 89, 90, 92, 95, 99, 100, 100, 101, 102, 103, 104, 106, 107, 107, 107, 108, 108, 109, 110, 110, 111
All other images from commons.wikimedia.org

Executive Editorial Team
Allen Quine
Wayne Hastings
Jeana Ledbetter
Byron Williamson

Developmental Editor
Randy Southern

Managing Editor
Christopher D. Hudson

Senior Editors
Mary Larsen
Jennifer Stair

Worthy Editorial
Kyle Olund
Leeanna Nelson

Design & Page Layout
Mark Wainwright,
Symbology Creative

Cover Design
Matt Smartt,
Smartt Guys design

museum of the Bible
BOOKS

WORTHY®
PUBLISHING

99 Astonishing Cities and Civilizations Found in the Bible

Introduction

From the beginning, we can see the biblical writers' emphasis on geography. In fact, the opening pages of the Bible, in the book of Genesis, give us an account of creation: an earth positioned in a vast universe, land and oceans placed below heavenly bodies, and a garden in "the east" (Genesis 2:8) with a river flowing out of it that separates into four rivers (Genesis 2:10–14).

As we read the rest of the Bible, we observe that it contains more than philosophy, theology, and pithy principles. The stories are filled with people who struggle with regional famines and sicknesses, who walk on dusty roads, who sail on seas, who conquer and rebuild cities. In this way, biblical principles are often integrated with significant geographic locations.

This book provides a panoramic view of some of these important locations, giving us the opportunity to deepen our knowledge of the characters and events in the biblical narratives.

Photos of the places where biblical narratives occur are presented alongside summaries of what the Bible says about these locations. As a result, this book can be enjoyed by those who want to learn more about the settings and context of the stories in the Bible.

CHAPTER ONE

Places of Notorious Deaths

Throughout the Hebrew Bible, we read stories about armies and individuals taking the lives of other people—whether through calculated military attacks or murderous impulses. While the biblical text doesn't always provide explicit reasons for people's violent actions, it often reveals the motivations behind some of these acts of violence. Seeking personal vengeance and fulfilling vows are two of these motivations. In this section, you'll read about the sites where some of the most notorious deaths in the biblical narrative occurred:

- Jericho
- Gilead
- Zaanaim
- Ashkelon

Left: Ruins in Tel es-Sultan, the site of ancient Jericho.

01 Jericho

Jericho was the site of one of the Israelites' greatest victories in Canaan. Located six miles north of the Dead Sea in the Jordan Valley, the city was renowned for its impenetrable walls. It is known as one of the oldest walled cities in the world. Yet those walls were no match for the army of Israel.

The battle plan was unusual. These were the tactical instructions from God to Joshua:

- Have your men march once around the city six days in a row.
- On the seventh day, march seven times blowing rams' horns and shouting. The walls will fall down.
- Rush into the city and kill every resident—except Rahab, who protected the two Israelite spies, and her household.
- Take no plunder from the city for yourself.

According to the book of Joshua (chapter 6), that's exactly what Joshua did.

However, booty from Jericho proved too great a temptation for an Israelite named Achan, who smuggled forbidden goods out of the city. The entire nation of Israel paid for his disobedience. During their next battle, the Israelites were routed by the much smaller forces of the city of Ai (see page 50).

> *By faith the walls of Jericho fell down after they had been encircled for seven days.*
>
> **HEBREWS 11:30**

When Joshua learned that God had punished his army because of Achan's crime, he and all the Israelites stoned Achan and his family to death and then burned their bodies, along with their possessions—including Achan's ill-gotten gains. The rogue Israelite paid dearly for the crime he committed in Jericho.

After its destruction, Jericho stayed uninhabited for nearly 400 years. People may have been put off by Joshua's curse in Joshua 6:26, which warned of dire consequences for anyone who tried to rebuild Jericho. Hiel of Bethel ignored the curse in the ninth century BC. He restored not only the city's buildings but also its walls. But he paid for it with the lives of his oldest and youngest sons (1 Kings 16:34).

According to the Gospels, Jericho also played a role in Jesus's ministry. It was in Jericho that Jesus healed Bartimaeus, a blind man (Mark 10:46–52); encountered Zacchaeus, a tax collector (Luke 19:1–10); and taught the parable of the ten minas (Luke 19:11–27).

Jericho is also where Herod the Great built a winter palace. Archaeological excavations have uncovered a magnificent structure that included a swimming pool, sunken garden, reception hall, and Roman bath.

The discovery of a series of burial caves—filled with mats, baskets, tables, stools, beds, boxes, bowls, combs, and beads—offers a glimpse of life during the time of the patriarchs (1900–1500 BC).

Today if you visit the site of this ancient city, you will see a ten-acre mound rising seventy feet above the surrounding plain. ∎

Top Left: Modern-day Jericho.
Top Right: Excavations of an ancient palace near Jericho.

(02 Gilead

Jephthah, a renegade warrior, became a judge of Israel after the people of Gilead recruited him to lead them in battle against their enemies, the Ammonites. Gilead was once Jephthah's home until a family dispute drove him away.

On the eve of the battle against the Ammonites, Jephthah vowed to God, "If you will give the Ammonites into my hand, then whatever comes out from the doors of my house to meet me when I return in peace from the Ammonites shall be the Lord's, and I will offer it up for a burnt offering" (Judges 11:30–31). Jephthah's daughter, his only child, was the first to walk out the door. Though devastated, he kept his vow to God. Whether he actually killed his daughter (the text does not explicitly say) or simply locked her away for the rest of her life as an "offering" is a matter of debate. Either way, he brought infamy to his homeland.

Gilead is Hebrew for a "heap" or "pile of stones"—an apt description for the mountainous region that stretched from the Arnon to the Yarmuk Rivers, between Bashan and Moab (located in modern-day Jordan). The King's Highway, one of the major trading routes of the ancient world, passed through Gilead. Those who controlled the region controlled the trade. Jephthah secured this revenue stream for the people of Gilead. ■

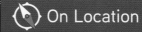 On Location

The Balm of Gilead

In his narrative poem "The Raven," Edgar Allan Poe writes as a young man who mourns the death of his beloved Lenore: "'On this home by Horror haunted—tell me truly, I implore—Is there—*is* there balm in Gilead?—tell me—tell me, I implore!' Quoth the Raven, 'Nevermore.'"

Poe is referencing a verse in the book of Jeremiah in which the prophet laments the decline and fall of the kingdom of Judah: "Is there no balm in Gilead? Is there no physician there? Why then has the health of the daughter of my people not been restored?" (8:22).

The balm of Gilead is thought to be an ointment made from resinous gum that was used for the healing of wounds.

Edgar Allan Poe, "The Raven" (1845).

Gilead grain fields near Listib, possibly Tishbe © BiblePlaces.com.

(03 Zaanaim

Sisera, the commander of the Canaanite army, terrorized Israel for twenty years with his division of iron chariots. His reign of terror came to an end when Deborah, a judge of Israel, and Barak, her appointed general, raised an army to rout the Canaanite forces. Of all the men in the Canaanite army, Sisera alone managed to escape the slaughter.

He fled on foot to the plain of Zaanaim (or perhaps the oak in Zaanannim) and hid in the tent of Jael, the wife of Heber the Kenite. Sisera believed he would be safe there because of a peace treaty between the Canaanites and the Kenites. He was gravely mistaken.

Jael welcomed Sisera into her tent and hid him under a blanket. But when the exhausted commander fell asleep, she hammered a tent peg into his skull.

The exact location of Sisera's murder is unknown. All we know is that it was near Kedeshin, the land allotted to the tribe of Naphtali. Its modern-day location is associated with Khan al-Tujjar, which lies about five miles west of the Sea of Galilee. ∎

Above: *Jael and Sisera* (1620), Artemisia Gentileschi (1593–1653),
© Everett Collection\Mondadori Portfolio.

04
Ashkelon

The deaths in Ashkelon were brutal. Samson, a judge of Israel renowned for his superhuman strength, was furious about losing a wager to his Philistine enemies in Timnah. He owed them thirty sets of clothing, and he knew just where to get them.

He traveled to Ashkelon, one of the five Philistine cities that were constantly at war with Israel. The narrative of Judges 14 suggests that Samson killed the first thirty men he saw there, stripped them of their clothes, and delivered the garments to the Philistines in Timnah.

The scene of this mass murder was a city on the Mediterranean coast, about twelve miles north of Gaza and about thirty miles south of modern-day Tel Aviv.

Its position on the trade routes from Turkey and Syria to Egypt made Ashkelon strategic for conquering. In its history, the city has been controlled by the Egyptians, the Philistines, the Phoenicians, the Israelites, the Assyrians, the Greeks, the Romans, the Persians, and the Crusaders, among others. ∎

Top: Fragment of ancient arch in National Park of Ashkelon, Israel.
Right: Silver-plated calf and pottery shrine, Ashkelon, sixteenth century BC.

SANCTAE CATHARINAE VIRGINI ET MART

CHAPTER TWO

Birthplaces and Hometowns

L*ike it or not,* the place you come from reveals something about you. Your hometown and culture invariably shapes your perspective and view of the world. Likewise, you often can't fully understand a person unless you know something about his or her origins, especially if that someone is a key figure portrayed in the Bible.

In the following tour of the birthplaces and hometowns of the Bible's most famous—and infamous—characters, we'll visit the following places:

- Haran
- Ephraim
- Valley of Sorek
- Ramah
- Gibeah
- Gath
- Sheba
- Tishbe
- Abel-meholah
- Uz

- Anathoth
- Gath-hepher
- Moresheth-gath
- Bethlehem
- Nazareth
- Bethsaida
- Tarsus
- Kerioth
- Capernaum
- Lystra

Left: The Church of the Nativity, Bethlehem.

O5 Haran

After leaving his hometown of Ur, the patriarch Abraham settled in Haran. After several years, at age seventy-five, he left Haran and finally completed his journey to Canaan (Genesis 11:31, 12:4).

Many years later, when Abraham wanted to find a wife for his son Isaac, he sent his servant to a region he knew well—Haran. Genesis 24 tells how Abraham's servant traveled to the land of Haran and found a suitable bride for Isaac by testing her generosity and service. The woman's name was Rebekah, and though she went to live with Isaac in his homeland, she never forgot her own.

Years later, Rebekah sent her son Jacob to Haran to find refuge after he incurred his brother's wrath for tricking him out of his birthright (Genesis 27:43). Jacob was traveling to Haran on another occasion when he had his famous dream of a ladder that reached to heaven (Genesis 28:10–15).

In the first century BC, Haran was an important business center in northern Mesopotamia. The name *Haran* means "parched," which offers a clue to the region's climate. Despite its dry climate, the region flourished with a good economy and political stability.

Haran was also a major center of worship for the moon god Sin (also called Nanna). The Babylonian king Nabonidus oversaw the rebuilding of the Sin temple there in the mid-sixth century BC.

The ruins of the city of Haran can be found in modern-day southeast Turkey and northern Syria. ∎

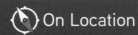

City of the Moon God

Genesis 11:31 tells us that Abraham's father, Terah, moved his family from Ur of the Chaldeans to Haran. Among those with him was his grandson "Lot the son of Haran." In Hebrew the spellings and meanings of *Haran* the brother of Abraham and *Haran* the city are different. The city was located on a main trade route, and the people of Haran worshiped the moon god Sin, as did the inhabitants of Ur. While we cannot be sure of Terah's motives for settling in Haran, the strategic location and similar religious practices are strong possibilities.

[Source: *The Lexham Bible Dictionary* (Bellingham, WA: Lexham Press, 2016); *Nelson's New Illustrated Bible Dictionary* (Nashville: Thomas Nelson, 1995).]

Above: Haran excavations from the northwest, © A.D. Riddle/BiblePlaces.com.

06
Ephraim

When the Israelites arrived in Canaan, the land was divided among the twelve tribes, a process that benefited some more than others. One of the key beneficiaries was Ephraim, the tribe named for Joseph's second son. The boundaries of Ephraim extended from the Jordan River to the Mediterranean Sea.

The region allocated to Ephraim was mountainous, which meant it could be easily defended. Yet it was also fertile, which made its inhabitants prosperous. Ephraim (a Hebrew word meaning "to be fruitful") was considered to be the heartland of Israel because of its abundant resources and desirable topography (Deuteronomy 33:13–17).

As the borders shifted over the years, Ephraim's territory—and importance—grew significantly. By the mid-eighth century BC, the prophets Isaiah and Hosea used the term *Ephraim* to refer to the entire northern kingdom of Israel. During the period of the judges, Ephraim was Israel's primary religious center. The tabernacle was located in Shiloh—a city in Ephraim—before being moved to Jerusalem during King David's reign (Judges 18:31; 1 Samuel 1:24). Israel's ancient worship centers of Bethel and Shechem were also located in Ephraim.

Several key figures hailed from Ephraim, including Jeroboam, the first ruler of the northern kingdom of Israel, and Deborah, the warrior and judge who led the Israelites against Canaan.

In 722 BC, the city of Ephraim, along with the rest of the northern kingdom of Israel, fell to the Assyrians. Its people were carried away into exile. ■

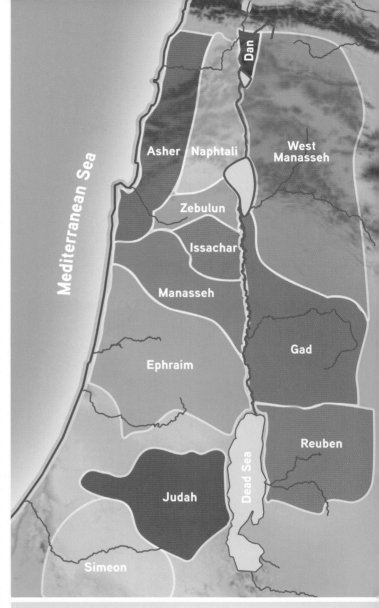

Right: Ruins of an ancient synagogue in the biblical Shiloh, Israel.

07 Valley of Sorek

The Israelite judge Samson was well known for his extraordinary strength and fighting prowess. On one occasion, he ripped apart a lion with his bare hands (Judges 14:5–6). On another, he killed thirty men in Ashkelon so he could take their clothes to pay off a bet (Judges 14:19; see page 11). And at Lehi, he single-handedly beat to death 1,000 Philistines using the jawbone of a donkey as his only weapon (Judges 15:14–15).

Yet against one enemy the legendary warrior was helpless. Her name was Delilah.

Delilah lived in the Valley of Sorek, which lay between the cities of Ashkelon and Gaza in southwestern Canaan. The region was originally allotted to the Israelite tribe of Dan. However, by the time of the judges (1200–1030 BC), it had fallen under Philistine control, and the people of Dan moved north. The valley separated the land of Judah from the land of the Philistines.

Samson loved Delilah, even though she lived among his enemies. Yet Delilah apparently didn't reciprocate his love. She conspired with Philistine rulers to trick Samson into revealing the secret of his strength—that razors had never touched his head due to his Nazirite vow (Numbers 6). As soon as his secret was out, the Valley of Sorek became the site of perhaps the most infamous haircut in history. While Samson slept, Delilah's coconspirators shaved off his long locks, rendering him as weak as any other man. He was taken prisoner, blinded, and forced to work as a slave for the Philistines until the end of his life.

Today the Valley of Sorek, where everything went wrong for Samson, is known as Wadi es-Sarar. ■

08 Ramah

Ramah (or Ramathaim-zophim, as it was also known) was located in the hill country of Ephraim (Judges 4:5; see page 15). A woman named Hannah lived in Ramah with her husband, Elkanah. In their culture, childlessness was considered a curse, and Hannah was taunted and shamed for her inability to bear children (1 Samuel 1:6). To make matters worse, she shared a home with her chief tormentor, Peninnah, her husband's other wife, who had already given him children.

Hannah traveled with Elkanah to the tabernacle at Shiloh. She prayed desperately for a son, vowing that if God would bless her with a son, then she would return him to the tabernacle for a life of religious service. Her prayers were answered. Back in Ramah, she gave birth to a boy and named him Samuel (1 Samuel 1:19–20).

True to her word, Hannah took young Samuel to the tabernacle and put him in the care of Eli, the chief priest. Samuel grew to be one of the most beloved prophets in Israel.

Samuel never lost sight of his roots in the hill country of Ephraim. According to 1 Samuel 7:17, he returned to Ramah frequently. He was even buried there (1 Samuel 25:1).

Many scholars identify Ramah with the New Testament city of Arimathea—best known as the hometown of Joseph, the wealthy secret disciple of Jesus who donated his own tomb for Jesus's burial (John 19:38).

The modern-day site of Ramah is located about five miles northwest of Jerusalem. ■

Left: *Samson and Delilah,* Anthony van Dyck (1599–1641).
Right: *Hannah Presenting Her Son Samuel to the Priest Eli* (ca. 1665), Gerbrand van den Eeckhout (1621–1674).

09 Gibeah

The name Gibeah *is a Hebrew word meaning "hill,"* but Gibeah is much more than just a city on a hill. Located in the land of Benjamin, about five miles north of Jerusalem, Gibeah served as the home base of Saul, the first king of Israel. From this city, King Saul reigned over the nation for thirty-eight years.

First Samuel 10 offers a telling glimpse of the city and its people. After being anointed king by Samuel, Saul returned home to Gibeah. The first people he encountered sneered at his new position and refused to acknowledge him as king (verses 26–27). That seems typical for the inhabitants of Gibeah. The city is rarely portrayed in a positive or even a neutral light in the Bible.

Consider Gibeah's notorious role in Israel's history before Saul ascended to the throne. According to Judges 19–21, Gibeah was the site of a brutal sexual assault in circumstances remarkably similar to those that brought down judgment on Sodom and Gomorrah. Outraged by the assault, several tribes of Israel gathered against Benjamin, the tribe responsible for the crime. The result was civil war, with Gibeah as its battlefield.

Today the location is known as Tel el-Ful. ∎

10 Gath

The Philistine city of Gath was one of the last remaining homes of the Anakites, a race of "giants" who plagued the Israelites during their conquest of Canaan (Joshua 11:22; 2 Samuel 21:20–22). The most famous of these giants was Goliath, the Philistine warrior who terrorized and humiliated Israel's army until a young shepherd named David, armed only with a sling and a handful of rocks, sealed his fate (1 Samuel 17:50).

Located on the coastal plain in southern Canaan, Gath was one of five city-states in the Philistine Pentapolis, a region notorious for its frequent military skirmishes with the Israelites. For a short time, Gath was home to the captured ark of the covenant (1 Samuel 5:8).

In a strange turn of events, while a fugitive from King Saul of Israel, David, the slayer of Goliath, befriended Achish, the king of Gath (1 Samuel 27:2–3). Their partnership proved to be short-lived, however, and Gath and Israel continued their mutual aggression. First Chronicles 18:1 reveals that David eventually, although temporarily, captured the city.

Gath was destroyed by the Assyrian king Sargon in 712 BC.

Because Gath was a popular name for cities in the ancient Near East, it is difficult to pinpoint the modern location of Goliath's birthplace. Some scholars identify it with Tel es-Safi. ∎

(11) Sheba

Sheba is the homeland of one of the most mysterious figures in the Hebrew Bible: the queen of Sheba. According to 1 Kings 10, she visited King Solomon in his palace to test his vaunted wisdom. She left with a favorable impression of not only Solomon's wisdom but also the wealth and splendor of his kingdom.

The question of where she came from has divided scholars for centuries. Where, exactly, is Sheba?

The Qur'an mentions the queen of Sheba's visit to Solomon and lists Sheba among the places that God destroyed. Muslim scholars identify it with South Arabia.

A recent British excavation has shed new light on this Bible story. Working from the theory that the kingdom of Sheba encompassed modern-day Yemen and Ethiopia, researchers discovered an ancient gold mine in that region, along with the ruins of a temple and the site of a battlefield. This may explain how the queen of Sheba was able to give vast quantities of gold to Solomon upon her arrival (1 Kings 10:10).

In the New Testament, Jesus calls her "the queen of the South," who "came from the ends of the earth to hear the wisdom of Solomon" (Matthew 12:42). ■

Top: *Visit of the Queen of Sheba to King Solomon*, Gates of Paradise, Baptistery of St. John, Florence, Italy.
Bottom: Ruins of queen of Sheba's palace, Aksum, Ethiopia.

12 Tishbe

In the ninth century BC emerged a prophet who dared to challenge the wickedness that had infected Israel's monarchy. This bold messenger confronted Ahab and Jezebel, the royal couple of the northern kingdom, about the Baal worship they instituted throughout the land and their blatant disregard for the Law of Moses.

The prophet was Elijah, whose name in Hebrew means "My God is YHWH" True to his name, Elijah waged a one-man war against the hundreds of prophets of Baal throughout the kingdom. His dramatic showdown with those prophets on Mount Carmel to prove his God was more powerful struck a decisive blow against idolatry in Israel (1 Kings 18).

Despite his status as one of the most beloved and revered prophets in Israel's history, little is known of Elijah's background. According to 1 Kings 17:1, he came from Tishbe in Gilead. Gilead was a mountainous region east of the Jordan River, teeming with forests, olive groves, and vineyards. The land was ideal for grazing animals. Its trees produced a sought-after balm in the ancient world (see page 9).

Identifying the location of Tishbe is more difficult. It is believed the modern-day site is somewhere near Mar Elias, a Byzantine church and monastery built during the sixth century AD to commemorate Elijah. ∎

13 Abel-meholah

How poetic is it that Israel's most beloved and revered prophet found his successor plowing a field? The name of the place where Elisha resided was Abel-meholah, a name that means "meadow of dancing."

First Kings 19:19–21 describes the encounter. Without a word, Elijah threw his cloak around Elisha. Undoubtedly, Elisha understood what the gesture meant because he immediately asked for permission to say good-bye to his parents. He then slaughtered his oxen that he had been using to plow, set fire to his equipment, cooked the meat, and used it to feed his friends and family. With the vestiges of his old life gone, Elisha left to follow Elijah and become his servant.

Abel-meholah, the place Elisha left behind, was a settlement in the tribal region of Issachar, west of the Jordan River and some ten miles south of the city of Beth-shean. The exact location of the city is disputed.

Aside from its status as Elisha's hometown, Abel-meholah is mentioned only in passing elsewhere in the

Hebrew Bible: as a destination of the Midianites when they were running from Gideon (Judges 7:22) and as the birthplace of the man who married King Saul's daughter Merab (1 Samuel 18:19). ∎

Top: Fresco of a prophet (ca. thirteenth century AD), Church of San Fermo Maggiore, Verona, Italy.
Right: *Elijah Ascends to Heaven in Chariot of Fire, with Elisha Below*, Padua, Italy.

14 Uz

The book of Job's self-contained story seems to exist apart from the rest of the Hebrew Bible. The same goes for its geography.

The book reveals its setting in its first sentence: "There was a man in the land of Uz whose name was Job." Scholars have difficulty pinpointing the modern location of Uz, and few clues exist in the Bible as to its geographical setting. Lamentations 4:21 associates the land of Uz with Edom, a region that stretched from the easternmost part of modern-day Egypt all the way to central Jordan. A scroll found among the Dead Sea documents suggests that Uz lay beyond the Euphrates River, possibly in Aram. Supporting this scroll is the genealogy of Genesis 10:23, which identifies a man named Uz as the son of Aram, a direct descendant of Noah.

While living in Uz, Job enjoyed wealth, possessions, a thriving family, and an unimpeachable reputation as a godly man—until his life suddenly spiraled downward.

As the tragedies mounted during Job's season of suffering, his friends in Uz questioned his godliness. Surely he had done something to anger God and bring down his judgment, they reasoned.

The narrative from the book of Job suggests that when his time of suffering ended, Job lived out his remaining years in Uz, enjoying his new family and newly restored riches. ■

15 Anathoth

The city of Anathoth lay three miles northeast of Jerusalem on a secondary road that ran from the capital to Bethel. As a Levitical town in the territory of Benjamin, Anathoth was set aside for members of the tribe of Levi, who were not given their own territory in Canaan.

The name likely comes courtesy of the Canaanites who inhabited the place before the Israelites arrived. Anat was the name of a Canaanite goddess.

The first verse of the book of Jeremiah identifies Anathoth as the prophet's hometown, though not many of its residents celebrated the association. Jeremiah is the embodiment of a prophet without honor in his own country. In fact, his own townspeople threatened to kill him if he continued to prophesy. In response, Jeremiah warned of God's judgment on the city (Jeremiah 11:21–23).

The Babylonian conquest and exile of Israel hit the city especially hard. Only 128 men returned to Anathoth after the exile. Today the site is called Anata. Ruins of the ancient city can be found a half mile southwest at Ras el-Kharrubeh. ■

Left: *Job and His Friends*, Ilya Repin (1844–1930), State Russian Museum. Above: Outside Anathoth, date unknown.

16 Gath-hepher

The prophet Jonah hailed from a border town in Israel named Gath-hepher. The town, whose name translates as "winepress of the well" (or "winepress of the digging"), marked an edge of the territory allotted to the tribe of Zebulun.

Gath-hepher's sole claim to fame in the Bible is its association with the wayward messenger of God. After Jonah's unsuccessful attempt to escape his prophetic duty, his adventure in the digestive system of a fish, and his bitter sojourn in Nineveh, Jonah returned to his hometown of Gath-hepher. Tradition holds that he is buried there.

The modern-day site of Gath-hepher is located near the Arab village of el-Meshed, about three miles north of Nazareth. The ancient ruins of the town can be found on a nearby hilltop, along with the purported tomb of Jonah. ■

17 Moresheth-gath

In the last decades of the eighth century BC, the prophet Micah left his home in the small town of Moresheth-Gath and traveled twenty-five miles southwest to deliver his prophecy to Jerusalem. His message was sadly familiar— and prescient. Because of Israel's wickedness, the nation would suffer devastating military defeat, and its people would be taken into captivity.

Little is known about the town Micah left behind, beyond its general proximity to Jerusalem. The name means "possession of Gath," so it was probably near in proximity to the city of Gath. It was probably also close to Mareshah (Micah 1:15) in the tribal territory of Judah, somewhere between Lachish and Achzib in the Shephelah region. Micah mentions towns and villages in both the Shephelah and Philistine country. ■

Left: Moresheth-Gath, ariel view from the east.

18 Bethlehem

The "little town" that figures so prominently in modern Christmas carols was, in Jesus's time, a nondescript community of probably less than 1,500 people. Perched on a ridge road about five miles south of Jerusalem, Bethlehem looks out over cultivated slopes to the west and desolate wilderness to the east.

Prior to the first millennium BC, Bethlehem was known for its proximity to the tomb of Rachel (Jacob's wife), a site sacred to the Jewish people. The city also plays a key role in the story of Ruth as Naomi's hometown, the place where she and Ruth settled after the deaths of their husbands.

The story of Ruth also sets the stage for Bethlehem's primary claim to fame. Ruth and her husband, Boaz, whom she met in Bethlehem, raised a son there named Obed. Obed raised a son named Jesse, who raised a son named David (Ruth 4:21–22).

David killed a Philistine warrior named Goliath (an unusually tall man, according to the text), wrote some of the most beloved psalms in the Bible, and succeeded Saul as the king of Israel. It's no wonder Bethlehem became known as the "city of David." It's the place he called home and where he was anointed king.

The prophet Micah predicted greater glory for the town. Micah 5:2 suggests that the long-awaited Messiah, the deliverer or savior of God's people, would come from Bethlehem.

Centuries later, when a Roman census required citizens to register in the city of their ancestors, a descendant of David named Joseph traveled to Bethlehem with his pregnant fiancée, Mary. The events that followed can be retold by anyone who's ever heard the Christmas story as told from the Gospel of Luke.

With no rooms available anywhere in Bethlehem, Joseph and Mary found shelter in a place that was likely used as a stable. And it was there that Mary delivered her child, laid him in a manger (a feeding trough), and named him Jesus.

The traditional site of Jesus's birth is a cave under the Church of the Nativity. Bitter disputes have arisen over the site and its markings.

The Roman emperor Hadrian destroyed the city in AD 135 in an effort to quell a Jewish rebellion. Some 200 years later, after the Roman Empire had embraced Christianity, Helena (the mother of Emperor Constantine) saw to the rebuilding of churches in Israel, including the Church of the Nativity in Bethlehem. After suffering severe damage, the church was rebuilt in the sixth century by Emperor Justinian.

Today Bethlehem is a Palestinian city in the West Bank with a population of about 25,000 people. ■

 On Location

The Date of the Birth of Jesus

According to the Gospel of Luke, Jesus was born "in the days of Herod, king of Judea" (Luke 1:5). Herod the Great, who ruled Judea between 37 and 4 BC, was still alive when Jesus was born in Bethlehem. Thus, the birth of Jesus could not have occurred after Herod's death in 4 BC.

The Gospel of Matthew states that when Herod received the "wise men from the east," he learned of the birth in Bethlehem of "he who has been born king of the Jews" (2:1–2). Determined to remove any threat to his rule, Herod "sent and killed all the male children in Bethlehem and in all that region who were two years old or under, according to the time that he had ascertained from the wise men" (verse 16). Assuming that Herod correctly calculated that Jesus was born up to two years earlier, this would put the birth of Jesus between 6 and 5 BC.

Above: View of Bethlehem.

19 Nazareth

After detailing the extraordinary events of Jesus's birth, the biblical narrative of his life goes virtually silent for thirty years. Little is known about the first three decades of his life, aside from the fact that he spent most of them in the hometown of his mother, Mary.

And if there was a place in first-century Israel where a person could live for thirty years in near anonymity, it was Nazareth.

Located in Galilee, the insignificant agricultural village was built on the steep slope of a hill about fourteen miles from the Sea of Galilee and about six miles west of Mount Tabor. The Via Maris, a major trade route to Egypt, could be accessed nearby. It is estimated that Nazareth's population during the time Jesus lived there was less than 500.

According to Luke 1:26–33, Nazareth is where the angel Gabriel first told Mary she would give birth to Jesus. This event is also known as the Annunciation. Other references to the village in the New Testament invariably involve Jesus and his ministry. The people of Nazareth rejected his message and even tried to kill him when he ministered there (Luke 4:28–30). As a result, Jesus moved the base of his operations to Capernaum. The village of Nazareth is not mentioned at all in the Hebrew Bible.

Right: Basilica of the Annunciation in Nazareth.   Below: View of Nazareth.

Opponents who mocked Jesus and his ministry seemed to find grist for their taunts in his association with Nazareth. A sarcastic comment found in the Gospel of John speaks volumes about the village's status. When the newly minted disciple Philip told his companion Nathanael that he was following Jesus of Nazareth, Nathanael replied, "Can anything good come out of Nazareth?" (1:46). Nathanael soon determined that the answer was a resounding yes and became a disciple himself.

Tradition holds that a Jewish-Christian community existed in Nazareth during the second and third centuries AD. In the sixth century, renewed interest in the Virgin Mary led to pilgrimages to the village. A group of pilgrims eventually founded the Greek Orthodox Church of the Annunciation near a freshwater spring known as Mary's Well. ∎

20 Bethsaida

At least one-quarter of Jesus's disciples spent their formative years in a small fishing village on the northwest shore of the Sea of Galilee, near where the Jordan River flows into it.

Simon Peter, his brother Andrew, and the lesser-known apostle Philip were born in Bethsaida. In John 12:20–22, when a group of curious Greeks wanted an audience with Jesus, they went to Philip. That may suggest that Philip had a certain rapport with Gentiles, perhaps from his upbringing in Bethsaida.

The exact location of this village, whose name is Hebrew for "house of the fisherman," is unknown. What is known is that the governor of the region (also named Philip) was politically savvy enough to give the village "city" status and rename it Bethsaida Julias, in honor of Caesar Augustus's daughter, sometime before 2 BC.

Bethsaida is where Jesus fed 5,000 men (plus an untold number of women and children) with five loaves of bread and two fish (Matthew 14:13–21). It's also where he restored a blind man's sight (Mark 8:22–25). Even after witnessing such extraordinary events, however, the people of Bethsaida rejected Jesus and his message.

Jesus addressed their unbelief with some blistering words in Matthew 11–22:

> Woe to you, Bethsaida! For if the mighty works done in you had been done in Tyre and Sidon, they would have repented long ago in sackcloth and ashes. But I tell you, it will be more bearable on the day of judgment for Tyre and Sidon than for you.

Tyre and Sidon were prosperous, Roman-occupied cities in the land of Israel. So Jesus was saying that unbelievers who had conquered and occupied Israel would have been more open to the message of Jesus than the residents of Bethsaida. ■

Above: Ruins and excavations of houses in the biblical village Bethsaida.

21 Tarsus

"I am a Jew, from Tarsus in Cilicia, a citizen of no obscure city" (Acts 21:39).

The apostle Paul was justifiably proud of his birthplace. The large, prosperous city on the Cydnus River (today known as the Berdan River) in the foothills of the Tarsus Mountains boasted an impressive pedigree.

The famed Roman orator Cicero served as governor of Tarsus in 50 BC. Nine years later, Mark Antony met Cleopatra for the first time in the city. Cleopatra's Gate, the entryway they used, still stands. Under Roman rule, Tarsus was named the capital of Cilicia, the fertile eastern plain region of Asia Minor.

The geography and location of the city played a major role in its development. Melting snow from the Tarsus Mountains flowed through the city to a lake five miles to the south. The lake served as both a naval station and a harbor. So even though Tarsus lay ten miles inland from the Mediterranean Sea, it thrived as a maritime center.

Major trade routes to central Asia Minor and Syria passed through Tarsus. The city was a melting pot of Greek and Asian culture. In the first century AD, its reputation as a cosmopolitan intellectual center surpassed even that of Alexandria and Athens. Some of the leading stoic philosophers of their day—including Zeno and Antipater—taught in Tarsus. ◼

22 Kerioth

Why was the apostle Judas called Iscariot? The question has divided scholars for two millennia. Some trace the origins of the name to the Greek word *sikarios*, which means "assassin." They suggest that Judas was part of a cadre of assassins dedicated to driving the Romans out of Judea.

Others opt for a more mundane, less nefarious interpretation: "man of Kerioth." Kerioth was a town in the mountains of Idumea, which lie west of the southern shore of the Dead Sea. If Judas was indeed from Kerioth, then he was the only apostle from Judea.

The prophet Amos refers to the "strongholds of Kerioth" in his prophecy against Moab (Amos 2:2). Joshua 15:25 connects Kerioth-hezron with the city of Hazor. The ruins of el-Kureitein, about ten miles south of Hebron, are believed to be those of Kerioth.

If Judas was a native of Kerioth, then he certainly brought no honor to his homeland. He served as treasurer for Jesus's ministry, yet John 12:4–6 suggests that he dipped into the treasury for his own purposes. His betrayal of Jesus to the Jewish Sanhedrin for thirty pieces of silver cemented his biblical infamy.

In some of the Gnostic literature, however, Judas is praised for his role in bringing about the destruction of Jesus's earthly body, which made the resurrection of the spirit possible. ◼

Above: Tarsus Waterfall, Turkey.   Middle: Silver stater minted in Tarsus, inscribed "Baal Tarsus."   Right: Doorway, Khirbet el-Qaryatein, Kerioth.

23 Capernaum

Capernaum played a key role in the early days of Jesus's public ministry. According to Matthew 4:13, after he was forced to leave his hometown of Nazareth, Jesus made Capernaum his base of operations in Galilee.

Located on the northwest shore of the Sea of Galilee, not far from the mouth of the Jordan River, Capernaum boasted a population of about 1,500 people at that time.

Andrew and his brother Simon Peter had moved to Capernaum from Bethsaida. James, his brother John, and the tax collector Matthew (also known as Levi) also called Capernaum home. And that's where Jesus found them.

Here are highlights of Jesus's ministry in the village:

- He healed—via long distance—a centurion's servant (Luke 7:1–10).
- He exorcised a demon (Luke 4:31–37).
- He cured Peter's mother-in-law of a fever (Luke 4:38–39).
- He caused a paralyzed man to walk (Mark 2:1–12).

As was the case in Bethsaida, the people of Capernaum rejected Jesus even after all they had seen him do and heard him say. And as was the case with Bethsaida, Jesus ended his association with Capernaum with a dire warning in Matthew 11:23–24:

> And you, Capernaum, will you be exalted to heaven? You will be brought down to Hades. For if the mighty works done in you had been done in Sodom, it would have remained until this day. But I tell you that it will be more tolerable on the day of judgment for the land of Sodom than for you.

Capernaum is usually identified today with Tell Hum. In the nineteenth century, a white limestone synagogue, dating from the fourth century, was uncovered in the region. Some scholars believe it is the same location of the synagogue where Jesus taught.

Archaeologists have also uncovered the remnants of a first-century home thought to be Peter's. ∎

Top: Synagogue in Jesus's town of Capernaum, Israel.

Middle: Excavated dwelling of what is believed to be the house of Peter.

 On Location

The House of Peter?

The Gospel of Matthew tells of a healing miracle that Jesus performed when he arrived at the town of Capernaum: "When Jesus entered Peter's house, he saw his mother-in-law lying sick with a fever. He touched her hand, and the fever left her, and she rose and began to serve him" (8:14–15).

Archaeologists have excavated several enclosed dwellings consisting of rooms surrounding a central courtyard in Capernaum.

The site was used for religious gatherings in the fourth century, and the names of Peter, Jesus, God, and Christ as well as liturgical expressions were found on the walls. Writing in AD 384, the Spanish nun Egeria related that the house of "the prince of the apostles" had become a church. A basilica—or pilgrimage site—was built over the site in the sixth century, the remains of which are still visible.

24 Lystra

The apostle Paul's visits to Lystra, according to the book of Acts, proved to be some of the most eventful of his entire ministry. The city, located in the rough-and-tumble region of Lycaonia, about twenty-five miles south of Iconium in central Asia Minor, was known for its temple dedicated to Zeus and its statue of Hermes, Zeus's son and messenger.

Paul and Barnabas made a memorable stop in Lystra on their first missionary journey around AD 48. In the course of their visit, Paul healed a man who had been disabled since birth. The townspeople who witnessed the healing convinced themselves that Barnabas was Zeus and Paul was Hermes and began to worship them until the two apostles put a stop to it (Acts 14:12–17).

Adoration quickly turned to rage when Paul's opponents came and stirred up the crowd. The people of Lystra stoned Paul and left him for dead—and then were amazed when he got up and returned to the city.

Paul returned to Lystra with Silas on his second missionary journey. That's when he recruited a young man named Timothy to join him in his travels.

Timothy was born to a Greek father and a Jewish Christian mother in Lystra. His mother, Eunice, and grandmother, Lois, known for their piety and faithfulness, taught Timothy from the Hebrew Bible. Timothy became a trusted confidante and fellow minister of Paul's.

The location of Timothy's hometown was a mystery until the 1885 discovery of an intact Roman altar inscribed with the city's Latin name, *Lustra*. The site of that discovery is in modern-day south-central Turkey. ■

Above: Remains of a stone structure, Lystra.   Right: Inscription found near Lystra.

CHAPTER THREE

Watery
Shortcuts

Because water is crucial to human existence, it's no wonder the word *water* appears hundreds of times in the Bible, starting at the beginning in Genesis 1. Water plays a prominent role in many miraculous stories of the Bible, including Jesus's turning water into wine, the spring that flowed from a rock during the Israelites' desert sojourn, and the morning dew that collected only where Gideon requested.

A few stories involve large bodies of water that defy the laws of physics to the benefit of certain people. In the pages that follow, we'll explore the sites where these events occurred:

- The Red Sea
- The Jordan River
- The Sea of Galilee

Left: View of the Red Sea from Sharm El Sheikh, Sinai, Egypt.

25 The Red Sea

The climax of the Israelites' nail-biting escape from Egypt takes place on the shore of the Red Sea. With Pharaoh's army bearing down on them, the people of Israel panic. Pinned against the sea's edge, they seem to have nowhere to go.

What happens next is not just the basis of one of the most iconic scenes in movie history (courtesy of Cecil B. DeMille's 1956 epic *The Ten Commandments*); it has also been the subject of a centuries-long debate among Bible scholars, who differ in opinion regarding where and how the waters "were divided" (Exodus 14:21).

The body of water we know as the Red Sea is a narrow inlet, roughly 1,400 miles long and 220 miles wide (though it narrows to 15 miles in some places). Situated between Africa and Arabia, the sea's northern end is split by the Sinai Peninsula into the Gulf of Aqaba on the east and the Gulf of Suez on the west. Its southern end narrows into the Bab el-Mandeb strait, which opens into the Indian Ocean. Historically, this strait is one of the most contested spots on the globe due to its importance to maritime trade with the East.

Many scholars take the Exodus account of what happened at the Red Sea at face value—that an eastern wind temporarily divided the water, allowing the Israelites to cross through the middle of the sea on dry ground, before the waters closed again on the Egyptian army, killing all of them. Other biblical scholars consider the Exodus account to be a myth—a legendary telling of the history of Israel.

Some people disagree as to the identification of the sea referred to in the Exodus account. The Hebrew word for *sea* does not distinguish between *sea* and *lake*. With that in mind, three possible routes have been suggested for the Israelites' escape:

- A southern route close to the Gulf of Suez
- A central route across the marshes of Lake Timsah (now part of the Suez Canal)
- A northern route across the narrow strip of land that divides Lake Bardawil (a saltwater lagoon) and the Mediterranean Sea

No consensus has been reached on any of the proposed routes. ■

Red Sea coastline in Ras Muhammad National Park, Egypt.

> It takes courage to attempt the impossible. What would we think of Moses today if when it was time to part the Red Sea, he had said, "Why don't you guys go build a bridge?"
>
> **—ANONYMOUS**

26 The Jordan River

The Jordan River, which flows for over 150 miles, forms a border between Israel and Jordan just south of the Sea of Galilee and between the West Bank and Jordan farther south until it reaches the Dead Sea.

Its waters provide a backdrop for many biblical events, including the ministry of John the Baptist and the baptism of Jesus. But the Jordan's most dramatic appearances in the Bible involve the parting of its waters.

As the people of Israel prepared to enter Canaan, led by the ark of the covenant, God offered them a glimpse of his power. According to Joshua 3:7–17, when the feet of the priests carrying the ark reached the overflowing waters of the Jordan, the river suddenly dammed itself upstream, allowing the Israelites to cross on dry ground.

Two similar bridgeless crossings of the Jordan are recorded in 2 Kings 2. The prophets Elijah and Elisha each divided the river by striking it with Elijah's cloak so they could walk across on dry ground. ■

Above: View of the Jordan River.
Right: *Jesus Christ Being Baptized by John the Baptist,* Arian Baptistery, Ravenna, Italy.

27 The Sea of Galilee

The harp-shaped freshwater lake located in the district of Galilee goes by many names in the Bible:

- Sea of Galilee
- Lake Galilee
- Sea of Chinnereth/Kinnereth (from the Hebrew word for a harplike instrument)
- Sea of Tiberias
- Lake of Gennesaret

Mentioned only as a border marker in the Hebrew Bible, the Sea of Galilee is the setting for many key events in the New Testament.

The lake lies some 700 feet below sea level and is surrounded by high hills, a geographic combination that makes it susceptible to abrupt temperature changes and sudden, violent storms. All of Jesus's disciples—especially the fishermen—likely had stories of white-knuckle experiences on the Sea of Galilee's waters.

However, those stories paled in comparison to what they witnessed one night when they were caught in a sudden storm. According to Matthew 14, the disciples were trying unsuccessfully to row against the wind when they saw a ghostly figure walking across the top of the water toward them.

Their (understandable) fears were calmed when they recognized the figure as Jesus. After crossing the Sea of Galilee as no one else had ever done, Jesus climbed into the boat. And immediately the storm stopped. ∎

On that day, when evening had come, [Jesus] said to them, "Let us go across to the other side." And leaving the crowd, they took him with them in the boat, just as he was. And other boats were with him. And a great windstorm arose, and the waves were breaking into the boat, so that the boat was already filling. But he was in the stern, asleep on the cushion. And they woke him and said to him, "Teacher, do you not care that we are perishing?" And he awoke and rebuked the wind and said to the sea, "Peace! Be still!" And the wind ceased, and there was a great calm. He said to them, "Why are you so afraid? Have you still no faith?"

MARK 4:35–40

Above and Below: Views of the Sea of Galilee.

CHAPTER FOUR

Where the
Dead Walk

For a handful of Bible characters in the Hebrew Bible as well as in the New Testament, physical death proved to be a short-lived condition. According to biblical texts, a number of men, women, and children from various walks of life miraculously regained consciousness after having been pronounced dead. The causes of their deaths and the circumstances of their resurrections vastly differ; yet in every account, the text makes it clear that actual death—not the appearance of death—preceded life.

In the pages that follow, we'll explore six cities in which graves could not hold their occupants:

- Zarephath
- Shunem
- Bethany
- Nain
- Joppa
- Troas

Left: Judean desert in Israel at sunset.

28 Zarephath

Around 863 BC, the prophet Elijah made his way to a port city on the Phoenician coast (in what is now Sarafand, Lebanon). Dwarfed on either side by the metropolises of Tyre and Sidon, the city of Zarephath was home to a widow whose name isn't given in the Bible but whose story of sacrifice and reward resonates even today.

Though the region at that time was gripped by a severe drought and famine, this woman offered hospitality to the venerable prophet. She fed him with what she thought was the last of her provisions. In return, her meager food supply miraculously multiplied. For the duration of the famine, her containers of flour and oil never went empty.

When the woman's son suddenly grew ill and died, Elijah covered the boy's corpse with his own body and prayed for God to restore the boy's life. Because the prophet's prayer was answered, the city of Zarephath holds the distinction as the site of the first recorded resurrection in the Bible.

In the ruins of the ancient city (also known as Sarepta), archaeologists have uncovered twenty-two kilns that date back to the thirteenth century BC. Excavations reveal that the residents of the city were skilled in pottery and metalworking, as well as in the production of olive oil and purple dye. ∎

Zarephath (now Sarafand, Lebanon) was a Phoenician city on the Mediterranean coast between Sidon and Tyre that had rich historical importance.

Above: *The Prophet Elijah and the Widow of Sarepta*, Bernardo Strozzi (1581–1644).

(29 Shunem

Shunem was a favorite destination of the prophet Elisha. The town at the foot of Mount Gilboa, on the southern border of Issachar's territory, was home to a wealthy (but childless) woman and her husband, who set up a room in their house for the prophet. To thank the woman for her hospitality, Elisha told her that her most fervent prayer would be answered: She would give birth to a son, even though her husband was very old.

A year later, the prophecy was fulfilled. The Shunammite woman gave birth to a son. Several years later, the boy grew suddenly ill and died on his mother's lap. The woman placed his body on a bed she had prepared for the prophet and set out to find Elisha. The prophet returned with her to the house in Shunem. After praying, Elisha stretched his own body over the boy's corpse two times. According to 2 Kings 4:35, the boy sneezed seven times and woke up. And Shunem became the second city mentioned in the Bible to host a resurrection.

The village also lends its name to the ancient practice of shunamitism, in which an elderly man would sleep with a virgin—usually in a nonsexual way. It was believed that a young woman's presence and warmth would provide much-needed vigor for a weak, aged man. Abishag, the young woman who served in that capacity for King David at the end of his life, hailed from Shunem (1 Kings 1:1–4).

The modern-day site is likely Solam, a small village surrounded by orchards and cactus hedges. ■

> *Now there came a day when Elisha passed over to Shunem, where there was a prominent woman, and she persuaded him to eat food. And so it was, as often as he passed by, he turned in there to eat food.*
>
> **2 KINGS 4:8, NASB**

Panoramic view from Mount Gilboa, Israel.

30 Bethany

Located on the eastern slope of the Mount of Olives, about two miles east of Jerusalem, the village of Bethany plays a key role in the narrative of Jesus's life.

Bethany is where Jesus was anointed in the home of Simon the leper. It's where he began his triumphal procession into Jerusalem for the Passover. It's also where his dear friends Mary, Martha, and Lazarus lived. The Bible doesn't say why Jesus connected so deeply with these siblings from Bethany, but modern research may offer a clue. According to literary evidence, the village was a place where the poor and sick—whose presence would make the inhabitants of Jerusalem ceremonially unclean—were welcomed and cared for. It stands to reason, then, that those who made Bethany their home did so for charitable purposes.

Jesus was some distance from the city when he received word that Lazarus was very ill. By the time he reached Bethany, his friend had been dead and entombed for four days. According to John 11, Jesus empathized with the mourners' sadness—and then instructed them to remove the rock from the opening of Lazarus's tomb. He called for Lazarus to come out. The mourners watched in wonder as Lazarus emerged from the tomb, still wrapped in his grave clothes.

The location of this extraordinary event is thought to be the current West Bank city of al-Eizariya, which translates as the "Place of Lazarus." A tomb, which has been identified as Lazarus's since the fourth century, can still be seen. A house dating from the time of Jesus still stands in the village. ◼

Jesus's Appearances in Bethany

- Jesus raises Lazarus
- Jesus begins his Palm Sunday journey from Bethany
- Jesus lodges in Bethany during the Passion week
- Mary anoints Jesus's feet with oil
- Jesus ascends to heaven from Bethany

Jesus said, "Take away the stone." Martha, the sister of the dead man, said to him, "Lord, by this time there will be an odor, for he has been dead four days." Jesus said to her, "Did I not tell you that if you believed you would see the glory of God?" So they took away the stone. And Jesus lifted up his eyes and said, "Father, I thank you that you have heard me. I knew that you always hear me, but I said this on account of the people standing around, that they may believe that you sent me." When he had said these things, he cried out with a loud voice, "Lazarus, come out." The man who had died came out, his hands and feet bound with linen strips, and his face wrapped with a cloth. Jesus said to them, "Unbind him, and let him go."

JOHN 11:39–44

Above: Lazarus, rising from the dead in the tomb. Studio shot of man wrapped in white cloth.

Bethany Church commemorating the home of Mary, Martha, and
Lazarus, as well as the tomb of Lazarus, Israel.

3⟩ Nain

Nain was a village in Galilee on the northwest slope of the hill of Moreh (or Little Hermon), about six miles southeast of Nazareth. The village is mentioned once in the Bible, but its appearance is a memorable one.

As Jesus approached the town gate, he encountered a funeral procession for the only son of a widow in Nain. Moved by the sight, Jesus touched the frame on which the body was being carried and commanded the young man to get up. The astonished mourners watched as the young man sat up and began talking, once again full of life. News of this great prophet spread quickly from the hillside village to people throughout Judea and beyond.

During the Crusades, Christian zealots built a church in Nain to commemorate Jesus's miracle. In the twelfth century, Nain became a Muslim village and remains one today. In the 1880s, the Franciscans acquired the ruins of the Crusade-era church and set to work rebuilding it. They were assisted by the Muslim head of the village, who allowed them to use all the water and stones they needed for the project.

Now called Nein, the village has a population of about 3,700 people. The ruins of the medieval church can still be seen. Several rock-cut tombs have also been uncovered nearby. What hasn't been found is evidence of a wall around the city. Scholars speculate that the "gate" mentioned in the Bible story (Luke 7:12) may have been simply a passageway between two houses. ■

Above: Ariel view of Nain.

32 Joppa

Joppa is the Greek name of the Israelite city Jaffa.
According to Acts 9, Joppa was the home of a godly woman named Tabitha who was known for her tireless work on behalf of the city's poor. Tabitha's sudden death devastated her large circle of acquaintances. When they heard that the apostle Peter was nearby, they sent for him.

Peter arrived at Tabitha's house, asked to be alone with her corpse, and then prayed over it. A short time later, he emerged with Tabitha, who was fully alive again.

Tabitha's resurrection is one of two biblically significant events that occurred in Joppa. While in the city, Peter had a vision of an enormous sheet being lowered from heaven. The sheet was filled with animals, some approved for consumption and some forbidden according to Jewish law. A voice commanded Peter to kill and eat the animals—the "clean" (approved) and the "unclean" (Acts 10:9–23).

That vision in Joppa marked a seismic shift in Christian history. Peter was being told to extend his ministry to Gentiles, who had been considered unclean—and therefore unacceptable—by Jews. From that point on, the message of Jesus was available to everyone.

The city also plays a key role in the Hebrew Bible. The cedar trees of Lebanon that were used to build Solomon's Temple in Jerusalem passed through the port of Joppa. When the prophet Jonah tried to run from his destiny in Nineveh, he sailed from Joppa.

Jewish rebels used the city as a base during Roman occupation, which twice made it a target for destruction by the Romans. The Jewish historian Josephus records that 8,400 people were killed in the first attack in AD 66.

Today the city is a suburb of Tel Aviv. ■

33 Troas

The apostle Paul visited the city of Troas twice during his missionary journeys. The first time, according to Acts 16:8–10, he saw a vision of man from Macedonia, inviting him to Europe.

Paul visited the city again around AD 56. According to Acts 20, during Paul's final sermon there, a young man named Eutychus took a seat on a windowsill three stories above the ground. When Paul got a little long-winded, Eutychus fell asleep and then fell to his death. The apostle rushed downstairs, threw himself on the lifeless man's body, and then announced that Eutychus was alive again.

Located on Turkey's west coast, this port city on the Aegean Sea was formerly named Antigona Troas (after its founder, Antigonus). It was later christened Alexandria Troas by Lysimachus, a Macedonian official who served Alexander the Great.

Remnants of the ancient city's wall can still be clearly seen. Excavations have also uncovered the remains of an ancient bath and stadium. ■

Left: Ancient port city of Joppa.   Above: Ruins of Troas.

CHAPTER FIVE

Enemy Territory

Ancient Israelites experienced both external and internal obstacles in their decades-long endeavor to permanently settle in the land promised to Abraham and his descendants. From the beginning of Israel's history—starting with Abraham—enemy nations, cities, clans, and tribes opposed God's people at almost every turn. Furthermore, the Bible records that the Israelites' seemingly endless pattern of wickedness and idolatry wreaked havoc on their nation. Their disobedience incurred the wrath of God, who allowed the people of Israel to suffer at the hands of hostile nations.

While the Bible names many enemies of Israel, in this section we'll take a look at five places where the Israelites most certainly were not welcome:

- Midian
- Moab
- Ammon
- Byblos/Gebal
- Bashan

Left: View of the Dead Sea and mountains of Moab from the Masada fortress, Israel.

34 Midian

Midian was the son of Abraham and Keturah. When Abraham expelled all potential rivals of Isaac, Midian, Isaac's half brother, was banished to "the east country" (Genesis 25:6). His descendants, the Midianites, forged a complex relationship with Isaac's descendants, the Israelites.

Isaac's grandsons conspired to sell their brother Joseph into slavery; the buyers were Midianite merchants (Genesis 37:28). Moses murdered an Egyptian; he spent forty years in exile among the Midianites (Exodus 2:11–15). Jethro, the priest of Midian, befriended him. He married Jethro's daughter Zipporah. His Midianite brother-in-law Hobab guided the Israelites in the wilderness (Numbers 10:29).

The mingling of the two nations proved costly for both. The influence of the Midianites on Israel was profound. Many Israelites switched their allegiance from the God of their fathers to idols such as Baal-Peor. At one point, God instructed Moses to assemble an army and destroy the Midianites (Numbers 25:16–18).

The Midianites didn't stay down for long, though. During the time of the judges, they emerged as one of Israel's chief oppressors. According to Judges 6, God called Gideon specifically to lead a military excursion against the Midianites.

Some scholars believe Midian was a coastal region on the eastern shore of the Gulf of Aqaba in the northwest Arabian Peninsula. Others believe that Midian was not a geographical place at all but rather a league of tribes. That would explain why Midianites pop up throughout the Bible in places like Sinai, Canaan, the Jordan Valley, and Moab. It would also explain why Midianite pottery has been discovered throughout the Middle East.

The discovery of the remnants of a Midianite tent-shrine in the Timna Valley of Israel has led scholars to suggest that the Midianites may have worshiped the Egyptian goddess Hathor, among other deities. ■

One day, when Moses had grown up, he went out to his people and looked on their burdens, and he saw an Egyptian beating a Hebrew, one of his people. He looked this way and that, and seeing no one, he struck down the Egyptian and hid him in the sand. When he went out the next day, behold, two Hebrews were struggling together. And he said to the man in the wrong, "Why do you strike your companion?" He answered, "Who made you a prince and a judge over us? Do you mean to kill me as you killed the Egyptian?" Then Moses was afraid, and thought, "Surely the thing is known." When Pharaoh heard of it, he sought to kill Moses. But Moses fled from Pharaoh and stayed in the land of Midian.

EXODUS 2:11–15

Above: Timna Valley, in the region of Midian.

35 Moab

Moab, Lot's oldest son, was the product of an incestuous relationship between Lot and his older daughter after the destruction of Sodom and Gomorrah. Moab's descendants settled in a mountainous strip of land that extended nearly the length of the eastern shore of the Dead Sea. The kingdom of Moab lay south of the kingdom of Ammon and north of the kingdom of Edom.

The Moabites were occasional allies of Israel. According to Deuteronomy 2:9, God gave explicit instructions to the Israelites to leave the Moabites in peace on their way to Canaan because he had given the Moabites their territory. So Moses negotiated safe passage through Moab. Shortly thereafter, Moses died and was buried in a valley of Moab (Deuteronomy 34:5–6).

Once the Israelites settled into Canaan, however, the relationship between the two nations soured. Judges 3 describes the brutal assassination of Moabite king Eglon by a left-handed Israelite from the tribe of Benjamin. A battle ensued between the Israelites and the allied nations of Moab and Ammon.

The main character of the book of Ruth is a Moabite widow who moved to Israel with her widowed mother-in-law and married an Israelite benefactor. Their descendants included David, the shepherd who gained notoriety by defeating the giant Philistine Goliath and becoming Israel's beloved king.

War between the nations continued under both Saul and David. The prophet Isaiah predicted the utter annihilation of the Moabites (Isaiah 15–16). History seems to confirm his prophecy. With the rise of the Persian Empire in the mid-sixth century BC, Moab disappeared from history.

Much of what we know about Moabite culture comes from the discovery of the Moabite Stone in 1868. The stone has a long inscription, dating from the ninth century BC, that has yielded a wealth of information about the Moabites' Hebrew-like language, as well as their history.

The modern-day Jordanian cities of Dhiban and Kerak are located in former Moabite territory. ■

The Genealogy of Shem

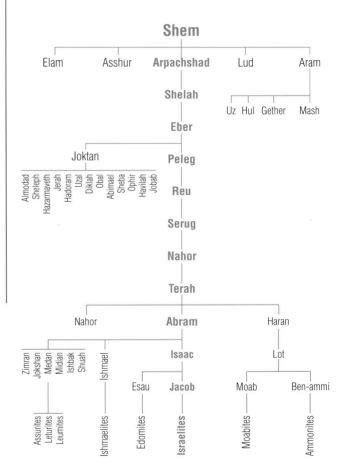

Left: Kerak Castle, a large crusader castle in Kerak (Al-Karak), Jordan, located in former Moabite territory. The Crusaders called it *Crac des Moabites* or "Karak in Moab."

36 Ammon

Like his half brother Moab, Ben-ammi was the product of an incestuous relationship—in this case, between Lot and his younger daughter. In Genesis 19:38, Ben-ammi is called "the father of the Ammonites." As a result, the Moabites and Ammonites are usually closely linked in the Bible. The kingdom of Ammon, which lay east of the Jordan River, bordered the kingdom of Moab on the north. Rabbah (modern-day Amman, Jordan), Ammon's capital city, was located at the headwaters of the Jabbok River.

Ammon's conflict with the Israelites began early in Israel's history. Sometime after the Israelites entered Canaan, they were defeated by a coalition of Ammonite and Philistine forces. An outcast named Jephthah eventually rallied Israel to victory.

First Samuel 11 describes an Ammonite threat to the Israelite city of Jabesh-Gilead. Saul assembled a fighting force 330,000 men strong and slaughtered the invaders.

Years later, David's scandalous relationship with Bathsheba began while his army was fighting the Ammonites. At the urging of his general, Joab, David led the final assault on Rabbah and a succession of other Ammonite cities, stripping them of their power and valuables along the way (2 Samuel 12:26–31). ■

37 Byblos/Gebal

In Psalm 83, the worship leader and prophet Asaph implores God to take action against Israel's enemies. He describes a confederation of groups plotting the destruction of the people of Israel. Among the conspirators he names in his prayer is the relatively obscure city of Gebal, also known as Byblos.

The city sits on a bluff in the foothills of Lebanon overlooking the Mediterranean Sea. It served as a key seaport in ancient Phoenicia. Residents of the city were renowned for their craftsmanship—some worked to cut stone and timber for Solomon's Temple (1 Kings 5:18).

Byblos, which lies approximately twenty-six miles north of modern Beirut in the Jbeil District of Lebanon, is a strong candidate for the world's oldest continuously inhabited city. It has been occupied without interruption since 5000 BC. For archaeologists, its layers of debris from thousands of years of habitation offer a treasure trove of information. The remains of well-built houses, dating from the Canaanite period, have been uncovered.

The longevity of the city may be attributed to its political flexibility. In the third millennium BC, at the height of Egyptian power, Byblos was an Egyptian colony. In the centuries that followed, the city aligned itself with Assyria, Persia, Greece, and Rome. In the Roman era, Byblos became a center for the cult of Adonis. ■

Top: Ammon citadel, Ammonite palace, 800 BC.
Left: Chalcolithic child burial jar, Byblos Museum.

38 Bashan

The Hebrew word Bashan **translates as "smooth, soft earth,"** which is an apt description for the region, inhabited by enemies of Israel, that consisted of fertile, grain-producing land. Bashan stretched from Hermon in the north to Gilead in the south and from the Jordan River on the west to Salcah (or Salekah) on the east. The region was renowned in the Bible for its mighty oaks (Isaiah 2:13), strong bulls and fattened animals (Psalm 22:12; Ezekiel 39:18), and rugged mountains (Psalm 68:15).

As the Israelites made their way to Canaan, the residents of Bashan determined to stop them. Led by King Og, the entire Bashan army marched out to battle the Israelites at Edrei. Og may have been one of the Rephaim, a race of giants who inhabited Canaan.

The Israelites weren't intimidated. Numbers 21:35 describes the outcome of the battle: "They defeated him and his sons and all his people, until he had no survivor left. And they possessed his land."

Bashan became part of the territory occupied by the tribe of Manasseh. Golan, a city of Bashan, became a city of refuge, where an Israelite who unintentionally killed another Israelite could find safety from revenge-seeking relatives of the dead person.

Around 860 BC, King Hazael and the Syrian army captured the cities of Bashan. According to 2 Kings 13:10–25, Jehoash, the king of Israel, recaptured Bashan after three battles with the Syrians—just as the prophet Elisha predicted. In the aftermath of those skirmishes, Bashan disappeared from history. Soon the name *Gilead* was used to refer to the entire region beyond the Jordan. ■

Above: Golan Heights and Mount Hermon from the south.

CHAPTER SIX

———

Lost
Cities

A *number of towns and cities* whose names are recorded in the Bible still exist today. Some of these places are thriving centers of religion or commerce; some consistently welcome throngs of tourists; some, however, are characterized by obscurity. Not all cities in the Bible have readily identifiable modern-day counterparts.

Some places that play a major role in the biblical narrative defied archaeologists' best efforts to uncover them for thousands of years. Some of them still remain lost. In the section that follows, we'll take a look at seven of these cities:

- Ai
- Ur
- Akkad (Accad)
- Antioch
- Nineveh
- Samaria
- Persepolis

Left: Hunting relief from palace of Assurbanipal in Nineveh, Assyria.

39 Ai

The book of Joshua traces the Israelites' conquest of the cities of ancient Canaan. The first, and perhaps most famous, battle in their march toward dominion of Canaan took place in Jericho. After utterly destroying that previously impenetrable city, the Israelites marched on to Ai, confident of a similar outcome.

Ai was one of the royal cities of Canaan. However, because of the insignificant military presence in the city, the Israelites sent only 3,000 soldiers to subdue it. What the supremely confident Israelite invaders didn't know is that someone in their midst—a man named Achan—had brought down God's wrath on the entire nation by taking forbidden plunder from Jericho (see page 8). As a result, the Israelites were routed. Thirty-six of their soldiers were killed in battle. The rest fled Ai thoroughly beaten and shaken.

That wasn't the end of the story for the Israelites. After making peace with God, they turned their attention back to Ai. This time, the entire Israelite army engaged in the battle. According to Joshua 8:28, "Joshua burned Ai and made it forever a heap of ruins, as it is to this day."

The Israelites succeeded in wiping Ai from the pages of history. Modern attempts to find the city have proved challenging. Many scholars have identified Ai with et-Tell, but the evidence is inconclusive. For one thing, excavation at that site has uncovered no signs of violent destruction. What's more, scholars believe the site had already been abandoned for hundreds of years when Joshua and the Israelites arrived.

These developments have led some researchers to shift their focus slightly to the west. Many now believe Khirbet el-Maqatir is the site of ancient Ai. Some scholars point to geographic, historical, and newly unearthed archaeological evidence of destruction in the fifteenth century BC to point to this location in the Jordan River valley. ∎

Above: Early bronze temple in et-Tell.

> Now the LORD said to Abram, "Go from your country and your kindred and your father's house to the land that I will show you. And I will make of you a great nation, and I will bless you and make your name great, so that you will be a blessing. I will bless those who bless you, and him who dishonors you I will curse, and in you all the families of the earth shall be blessed." So Abram went, as the LORD had told him, and Lot went with him. Abram was seventy-five years old when he departed from Haran. And Abram took Sarai his wife, and Lot his brother's son, and all their possessions that they had gathered, and the people that they had acquired in Haran, and they set out to go to the land of Canaan.
>
> GENESIS 12:1–5

The city of Ur is of vital importance to the history of Judaism, Islam, and Christianity. According to Genesis 15:7, the patriarch Abraham originally hailed from Ur. At its zenith, the port city on the Euphrates River was renowned as a center of trade, religion, and learning. Ships came from as far away as India to partake of its goods and marvel at the enormous ziggurat that towered over the city. The Sumerian people of Ur revered many gods, but the moon god Sin received most of their attention and worship.

For 2,000 years, Ur reigned as the preeminent city of ancient Sumer (in southern Mesopotamia). And then a strange thing happened: The Euphrates started to shift its course. The former coastal city found itself landlocked. By 450 BC, the city lay several miles inland. Without ports to fuel its economy, Ur gradually faded into oblivion.

Buried by the unforgiving sands of the region, the city lay hidden for over 2,500 years. It wasn't until after World War I that archaeologists discovered the extent of the ruins that survived. These ruins are in Tell al-Muqayyar, Iraq. ∎

Left: *Abraham* (1857), fresco by Joseph Schönmann (1799–1879).
Right: Clay nail with inscription of Ur-Nammu (ca. 2113–2096 BC), Ur. **51**

41 Akkad/Accad

The story of empires and their impact on history begins with Akkad (also spelled Accad), a city-state that grew into a superpower in a very short period of time. At its height, the Akkadian Empire stretched across ancient Mesopotamia, from the Persian Gulf to the Mediterranean Sea and up into Asia Minor.

For a century and a half, Akkad served as the hub of the most powerful economic and political force in the world. Literature, art, and science flourished within its borders. The city is mentioned in Genesis 10:10 as one of the political centers of the warrior-king Nimrod. Akkad also features prominently in hundreds of ancient cuneiform tablets.

Yet the location of this capital city has been lost to history. Scholars have searched for its remains along the Tigris and Euphrates Rivers and in various sections of modern Baghdad, among other places—all to no avail. Barring a near archaeological miracle, historians may never uncover the secrets of the world's first capital.

The clues that have been found are tantalizing, though. Various excavations of the vicinity where Akkad may have been located reveal a sudden and complete abandonment of the region near the end of the third millennium BC. Many scholars believe a severe, centuries-long drought prompted the evacuation. ∎

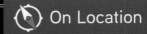

On Location

Priestess of Mesopotamia

An Akkadian woman held the highest religious office of the two most significant centers of the Sumerian-speaking regions of Mesopotamia. Enheduanna, an accomplished poet and proficient writer, was the high priestess of the moon god Nanna (also called Sin) at the city of Ur. She eventually became the high priestess of the sky god Anu at Uruk.

Above: Sumerian brick stamp of Sar-kali-sarri, king of Akkad.

Above: Sumerian marble tablet dedicated to Enimmu, belonging to Rimush, king of Akkad.

42 Antioch

Antioch was founded in 300 BC by Seleucus I Nicator, a general of Alexander the Great. Located on a bend of the Orontes River, some 300 miles north of Jerusalem, Antioch served as the capital of the Seleucid Empire until AD 64 and once boasted a population of more than 500,000 people—an unusual amount, considering very few ancient cities were that large. Key features of the city included aqueducts, amphitheaters, and Roman baths.

In the first century, the city was home to a thriving Jewish community, which made it a natural launching pad for Christianity. According to Acts 11, Antioch was the site of the first Gentile church, as well as the place where Jesus's followers were first referred to as Christians. The apostle Paul launched three of his missionary journeys from the city.

Antioch isn't "lost" in the normal sense. Scholars know where its ruins lie: just outside Antakya, in modern-day Turkey. Thanks to centuries of erosion near the Orontes River, however, they are buried under a thick layer of mud. That's why evidence of Antioch's most magnificent structures, including the Imperial Palace and Constantine's Great Church, has yet to be discovered. Compounding the problem is urban sprawl in northern Antakya. Acres of small ruins have been leveled and built over. ■

Church of Saint Peter, Antioch, Turkey.

43 Nineveh

Nineveh lies at the heart of one of the most famous (and ill-advised) personal rebellions against God in the Bible. God instructed the Hebrew prophet Jonah to take a warning to the city in Upper Mesopotamia: Repent or be destroyed. Instead, Jonah took the first ship heading in the opposite direction—not because he was afraid of the Ninevites, but because he was afraid they would repent and be spared by God.

Such was Jonah's hatred for the great Assyrian city that he risked his own standing with God to hasten its destruction. The rest of Jonah's story is well known. After being thrown overboard from his ship, the prophet was swallowed by a great fish and deposited back on land after three days. And when he finally fulfilled his prophetic duties in Nineveh, Jonah's worst fears were realized. The people of Nineveh sincerely repented of their wickedness and were spared by God—temporarily (see the book of Nahum).

Nineveh was an extraordinary city by any ancient measure. Its location on the Tigris River featured prominently in its infrastructure. Canals crisscrossed its streets. Its entrances were marked by fifteen elaborate gates. Its library boasted one of the largest collections of scrolls in the ancient world. And towering over it all was a palace unlike any that had been built before.

Opulence is no substitute for protection, however. In 612 BC, Nineveh was obliterated from history. Even its foundations were destroyed. Centuries of biblical prophecy were fulfilled in its demise (Nahum 1:8; Zephaniah 2:13–15). The city stayed lost for almost two millennia—until the 1840s, when archaeologists finally discovered the site of the Assyrian capital just across the Tigris from modern-day Mosul, Iraq. Researchers have since uncovered extensive ruins on the site. ■

Above: Ancient Assyrian relief.
Right: *Jonah Preaching to the Ninevites*, Gustave Doré (1832–1883).

44 Samaria

Around 920 BC, Omri, the king of Israel, built the city of Samaria on a flat-topped hill that rose from a wide, basin-shaped valley about thirty miles north of Jerusalem and six miles northwest of Shechem. Omri bought the hill from a man named Shemer, whose name forms the basis of the city's name (1 Kings 16:23–24).

The city boasted an assortment of impressive public buildings and royal residences. Soon after its construction, Samaria was named the capital of the northern kingdom of Israel, which consisted of ten of the twelve tribal regions.

In the Hebrew Bible, Samaria is notorious for its corruption and idolatry. The evil King Ahab built for himself a palace made of ivory in the capital city, along with a temple to the Canaanite god Baal. Samaria features prominently in several prophecies that urge its repentance and warn of its destruction. But the warnings ultimately went unheeded.

In 721 BC, some 200 years after it was built, Samaria was conquered and destroyed by the Assyrians, establishing a pattern for the city that would continue for centuries. After an extensive rebuilding project, the city was destroyed again—this time by Jewish forces—around 109 BC. Under Roman rule, the city was rebuilt, destroyed again, and rebuilt again.

In the aftermath of so much reconstruction and deconstruction throughout the centuries, traces of the original city vanished under the debris. It wasn't until the early twentieth century that archaeological excavations uncovered vestiges of the once-majestic Israelite capital. ■

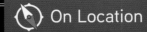

On Location

The Parable of the Good Samaritan

In the parable of the good Samaritan, Jesus admonished those who had a prideful attitude of superiority toward others. In the parable, two respected authority figures in Jewish life, a Levite and a priest, refused to aid a man who had been robbed and left for dead along the road. By contrast, a Samaritan who was passing by stopped to bind up the man's wounds and helped transport him to an inn where he could receive further assistance. Jesus blessed the Samaritan, which would have offended many first-century Jews, who looked down upon Samaritans as second-class citizens. The Samaritans were believed to be Jews who had intermarried with Gentiles and thus were not of pure Jewish descent. Jesus's disciples realized that the hated Samaritan had been a good neighbor, and Jesus instructed them: "You go, and do likewise" (Luke 10:37).

Samaria from the north.

45 Persepolis

Scholars believe it was the Persian emperor Cyrus the Great who, in the sixth century BC, chose a mountaintop location (in what is now Iran) for a city he wanted built. The mountain's peak had to be leveled before construction could begin. The city that resulted was Persepolis, the future capital of the Persian Empire. And while Cyrus made the city a reality, his successor, Darius I, made it memorable.

Persepolis gained notoriety in its day for its wealth and splendor. Darius ordered the construction of an ornate palace made of white marble and black stone (and featuring doors made of gold and other precious metals)—as well as a treasury; a council hall; the Apadana, a large hall supported by seventy-two columns; and a dual, symmetrical stairway that led to the city's terrace. Elaborate statues dotted the landscape.

Darius made the city his royal residence, but he soon discovered the challenges of trying to run an empire from a remote location, away from the trade centers and political hotspots of the day.

The remoteness of Persepolis's location would explain why the Greeks seemed to be unaware of its existence until Alexander the Great discovered it in 330 BC. After surveying the city's astonishing architecture and opulence, the great conqueror burned the city to the ground. The inferno was so intense and the destruction so complete that nothing was left standing.

A mere 200 years after its construction, Persepolis was no more. The site was abandoned, and Persepolis disappeared from history for 2,000 years. It wasn't until the seventeenth century that scholars pieced together the origin of the charred pillars and other ruins that lay about thirty-five miles northeast of Shiraz, Iran. ■

Above and Right: Ruins of ancient Persepolis, capital of Achaemenid Empire near Shiraz, Iran.

CHAPTER SEVEN

"Woe unto You": Places Targeted by Prophets

If you were a citizen of the ancient world, *woe* was the last word you wanted to hear in conjunction with your city. *Woe* was a declaration of God's anger. *Woe* signified a curse—a promised act of punishment—directed at people who were guilty of disobeying God's commandments. *Woe* was a warning of impending judgment. *Woe* meant life would never be the same again.

In the pages that follow, we'll explore six cities whose residents found themselves on the business end of a biblical prophet's (literal or figurative) *woe*:

- Babylon
- Damascus
- Hazor
- Jerusalem
- Edom
- Tyre

Left: Skyline of Jerusalem.

46
Babylon

According to Genesis 10:8–10, Babylon was founded by Nimrod, the great-grandson of Noah. The site establishes its notoriety a chapter later in the Bible as the place where humans tried to build a tower (or ziggurat) that would reach the heavens. According to the Genesis narrative, God confounded the workers' efforts by confusing their language. The resulting name of the place, Babel, reflects that confusion (and forms the root of *Babylon*).

After Genesis 11, Babylon disappears from the Bible until the prophets Isaiah, Jeremiah, Ezekiel, and Daniel reveal God's plan for the city. Isaiah speaks of the conquering of Babylon (13:17–19) by the Medes and the Persians in the sixth century BC.

In the earlier part of the sixth century BC, the Babylonians boasted control over much of the ancient Near East. It was during this time that Nebuchadnezzar's forces attacked Jerusalem and carried many of its citizens to Babylon.

According to the ancient historian Herodotus, at its peak the city of Babylon was laid out as a fourteen-mile square, with the Euphrates River running north to south

> And the LORD came down to see the city and the tower, which the children of man had built. And the LORD said, "Behold, they are one people, and they have all one language, and this is only the beginning of what they will do. And nothing that they propose to do will now be impossible for them. Come, let us go down and there confuse their language, so that they may not understand one another's speech." So the LORD dispersed them from there over the face of all the earth, and they left off building the city. Therefore its name was called Babel, because there the LORD confused the language of all the earth. And from there the LORD dispersed them over the face of all the earth.
>
> GENESIS 11:5–9

through the middle of it. The city was protected by inner and outer walls that Herodotus estimated were 350 feet high and 87 feet thick. Inside the walls, Babylonians lived in spacious houses and enjoyed amenities such as the Hanging Gardens, one of the seven wonders of the ancient world.

With storehouses stocked with enough supplies to withstand a twenty-year siege, Babylon seemed invulnerable. Cyrus the Great of Persia, however, conquered the city in 539 BC. Two centuries later, part of the city suffered destruction at the hand of Alexander the Great. And in 261 BC, Antiochus I left Babylon in ruins. ∎

Panorama of Babylon ruins, Hillah, Iraq.

47 Damascus

"Behold, Damascus will cease to be a city and will become a heap of ruins" (Isaiah 17:1). Ironically, the city of Damascus is singled out in Isaiah 17 not for its opposition to Israel but for its affiliation with Israel. The northern kingdom of Israel is the primary target of God's wrath in the passage. Damascus, the capital of Syria, had joined forces with Samaria, the capital of the northern kingdom, against the southern kingdom of Judah. So the Syrian city's inclusion in Isaiah's destruction language was due to guilt by association.

In the ancient world, Damascus occupied an enviable position near the trade routes that connected Mesopotamia, Egypt, and Arabia. Its strategic location on the Barada River, northeast of Mount Hermon, also accounts for its prominence as a cultural and religious center.

In the New Testament, Damascus is perhaps best known as the place where Saul of Tarsus's career as an enemy of Christianity came to an abrupt end. According to Acts 9, the future apostle Paul was on his way to Damascus to arrest Christians there when Jesus appeared to him in a blinding light and forever changed the course of his life.

In the Hebrew Bible, though, Damascus is the target of God's judgment. Second Kings 16:9 records as history the words of Isaiah, when Tilgath-Pileser III, the king of Assyria, destroyed the city and carried away its inhabitants. The city was rebuilt. Some claim that Damascus has been destroyed—and rebuilt—more often than any other city in history.

Today Damascus is Syria's capital and largest city. ▪

Above: People in a central square in pre-war Damascus, Syria.

48 Hazor

In Jeremiah 49:28–33, the prophet warns the people of the kingdoms of Hazor to take shelter in the deepest caves they can find. That, according to Jeremiah, was their only hope for escaping the instrument of God's wrath: Nebuchadnezzar, the king of Babylon.

Little is known about the kingdoms of Hazor (which should not be confused with the town of the same name in Israel). Some scholars have suggested that they may have occupied a region in the Arab Desert east of the Jordan River.

Jeremiah recognized that his words would fall on deaf ears because the people of Hazor were confident in their safety and protection. Jeremiah also understood that the Hazorites would learn too late just how vulnerable they were.

The destruction that awaited them at the hands of the Babylonians would be complete. "Hazor shall become a haunt of jackals, an everlasting waste; no man shall dwell there; no man shall sojourn in her" (Jeremiah 49:33). ■

49 Jerusalem

Any discussion of the most important cities in the Bible must include Jerusalem. Likewise, any discussion of the key cities of Islam and Judaism must also involve the city of Jerusalem.

Perhaps no other city in human history has been more contested. Israelis and Palestinians both lay claim to it as their capital. And perhaps no part of Jerusalem has been more prone to disputes than the Temple Mount (Haram esh-Sharif), a hill located in the Old City of Jerusalem. In Judaism, the site is associated with Mount Moriah (the place where Abraham nearly sacrificed his son Isaac) and Mount Zion.

Even more significant is Jerusalem's role as the center of Jewish worship during the temple eras. Scholars believe the first Jewish temple, built by King Solomon in 957 BC, stood on the Temple Mount. (Because of political sensitivities and the sacred nature of the site, archaeological excavations there have been extremely limited.) That structure was completely destroyed by the Babylonians in 586 BC.

Work on a second temple began less than fifty years later. Led by the governor Zerubbabel, the construction of this phase—the Second Temple—was completed in 516 BC. The temple was dedicated a year later.

Nearly 500 years after that (ca. 20 BC), Herod the Great, the Idumaean puppet king of Judea, initiated a massive expansion and reconstruction of the temple. Herod's aim was to secure his place in history by commissioning a variety of building projects in an attempt to court favor with both the Jews and Romans.

During Jesus's lifetime, the temple was a work in progress; but its majesty and sheer enormity drew worshipers and curiosity seekers from all over. Jesus's disciples were not immune to the grandeur and spectacle of the temple project. When one of Jesus's followers asked Jesus to comment on the temple's splendor, though, he received an answer he didn't expect. According to Mark 13:2, Jesus said to him, "Do you see these great buildings? There will not be left here one stone upon another that will not be thrown down." The project was still more than thirty years from completion, and Jesus was already predicting its demise! Jesus's vivid description of "not one stone" being left on top of another reads like a playbook for the Roman warrior Titus, who utterly destroyed the Jerusalem temple in AD 70. ■

Above: Tower of David, Old City, Jerusalem.

50 Edom

The kingdom of Edom bordered Judah, the Dead Sea, and Moab on the north and extended all the way to the Gulf of Aqaba. Also known as Idumea, the region was wild and rugged—appropriate, since its founder was Esau, the wild and rugged brother of Jacob.

As the Israelites made their way to Canaan, the Edomites refused to allow them passage through their land. That initial encounter set the tone for the subsequent relationship between the two nations. King David conquered Edom during his reign, as did King Amaziah years later. Yet Edom regained its independence and continued to wage war against its enemies to the north. As the Israelite kingdoms grew weaker, Edom asserted itself more. Eventually the Edomites invaded and occupied southern Judah.

The prophets Isaiah, Jeremiah, Ezekiel, Joel, Amos, Obadiah, and Malachi all delivered messages against Edom. Messages of Edom's abandonment and desolation eventually proved to be prescient.

The nation and its capital city of Petra (see page 70) were overrun by other Arab groups in the fifth century BC. Those groups were conquered by the Nabataeans around 312 BC. The Nabataeans were conquered by the Romans in AD 106. The Roman conquest signaled the beginning of the end for Edom. For over 500 years (the seventh to the twelfth centuries AD), the nation was abandoned and desolate. ∎

Above: Horvat Qitmit, Edomite pottery head of goddess, late 7th–early 6th century BC.

Above: View of Arabah and mountains of Edom from Mount Ayit.

51 Tyre

According to Greek mythology, the city of Tyre was the birthplace of Europa (who gave Europe its name) and Dido (who fell in love with Aeneas). This ancient Phoenician port city on the Mediterranean Sea was actually two cities in one. Tyre's main trade center was located on an island; the "old" city (known as Ushu) lay about a half mile away on the mainland. The name *Tyre* means "rock."

Over time, the island portion of the city grew more prosperous and populated than its mainland counterpart. Heavy fortifications were built to protect it. Nebuchadnezzar II of Babylon discovered just how effective those defenses were when he laid siege to Tyre for thirteen years in the sixth century BC. He was unable to break the city.

The people of Tyre were known for their skills in working with a certain purple dye that came from shellfish. Because purple was the color of royalty in the ancient world, the Tyrians' work was highly prized. As a result, they enjoyed a certain measure of wealth and prestige.

Tyre entered into an alliance with King David and Israel that benefited both parties tremendously. However, years later when Jerusalem fell, the people of Tyre saw an opportunity to increase their share of trade. Tyre's citizens reveled in Jerusalem's destruction—an attitude that, according to Ezekiel, angered God. Ezekiel wrote of punishment for Tyre's treachery (Ezekiel 26–28).

Some theologians point to the siege and attack led by Alexander the Great in the fourth century BC as the fulfillment of Ezekiel's prophecy. Like the inhabitants of other cities in the region that fell to the Macedonian conqueror, the people of Tyre surrendered to Alexander. But because they refused to allow him to make a sacrifice to their god inside the city, he built a causeway between the mainland and the island fortress that allowed him to breech Tyre's walls, destroy the city, and slaughter thousands of its inhabitants. As sediment collected around Alexander's man-made causeway in the centuries that followed, the island became connected to the mainland.

Today Tyre is located in Lebanon, about twelve miles north of its border with Israel. ∎

On Location

Royal Purple

In the ancient world, the color purple was costly to produce. Therefore, it was associated with elegance and wealth. The dye was made from the rare murex snail, which is native to the eastern Mediterranean. Each snail yielded only a pinprick of deep purple pigment, and thousands of snails were required to produce a single gram of the superior waterproof and permanent murex dye.

Tyre was the capital of the Phoenicians, a seafaring people who controlled the production of royal purple. When King Solomon was building the temple, he asked King Hiram of Tyre to send artisans "skilled to work in gold, silver, bronze, and iron, and in purple, crimson, and blue fabrics" (2 Chronicles 2:7).

Above: Tyre, Al-mina archaeological site, with Roman rectangular theater vault.

CHAPTER EIGHT

The Name Says It All

Similar to personal names, the names of geographic places hold significance for many different reasons. Throughout the Bible, we encounter places—including cities, valleys, gardens, fields, wells, bodies of water, and even rocks—that were named to commemorate important people or meaningful experiences. Some names we skip over without much thought, but some place names in the Bible are so vivid, so descriptive, that they demand to be explored further. In the brief section that follows, we'll take a look at three such locations:

- The Valley of Dry Bones
- Golgotha (Place of a Skull)
- Petra (Rock)

Left: The Treasury (Al-Khazneh), Petra, Jordan.

52 The Valley of Dry Bones

During the siege of Jerusalem around 597 BC, Ezekiel was exiled to Babylon, where he enjoyed a certain measure of freedom among his fellow Jewish exiles. It was from his Babylonian place of exile that the prophet was transported—whether physically or in a vision—to one of the strangest places recorded in the Hebrew Bible: a valley of dry bones.

The location of this valley is impossible to determine. The only descriptive feature Ezekiel offers is that the floor of the valley was covered with very dry bones. According to Ezekiel 37, God instructed Ezekiel to prophesy to the bones. As he did, they began to reanimate. The bones came together, followed by flesh, skin, and finally the breath of life.

The valley of dry bones became the valley of a vast army of living people. God explained to Ezekiel that the bones symbolized Israel, which was in a state of living death in exile. The reanimation represented the future of the nation—specifically, God's plan to restore the people of Israel back to their homeland, to bring them out of the valley of dry bones. ■

The hand of the LORD was upon me, and he brought me out in the Spirit of the LORD and set me down in the middle of the valley; it was full of bones. And he led me around among them, and behold, there were very many on the surface of the valley, and behold, they were very dry. And he said to me, "Son of man, can these bones live?" And I answered, "O LORD GOD, you know." Then he said to me, "Prophesy over these bones, and say to them, O dry bones, hear the word of the LORD. Thus says the LORD GOD to these bones: Behold, I will cause breath to enter you, and you shall live. And I will lay sinews upon you, and will cause flesh to come upon you, and cover you with skin, and put breath in you, and you shall live, and you shall know that I am the LORD."

EZEKIEL 37:1–6

53 Golgotha
(Place of a Skull)

Many Christians point to the crucifixion as the darkest day in human history—spiritually and literally. According to Matthew 27:45, darkness covered the land for three hours while Jesus hung on the cross.

An event loaded with such seismic implications and unimaginable suffering requires a suitably foreboding location—and finds it in Golgotha, which means "Place of a Skull" (Matthew 27:33). Some believe the name refers to the shape of the rock formation—the hill of Golgotha resembled the top half of a human skull. Others suggest that the skulls and remains of other crucifixion victims were scattered about the hillside. Still others contend that the name derives from a neighboring cemetery.

Some people believe Golgotha was near enough to the gate of Jerusalem that people coming and going from the city could see the inscription on Jesus's cross, which said, "Jesus of Nazareth, the King of the Jews" (John 19:19). The public spectacle of crucifixion was the Roman Empire's way of reminding its citizens what happened to those who challenged its authority.

In the fourth century AD, the Roman emperor Constantine built the Church of the Holy Sepulchre around the site traditionally associated with Golgotha. ■

Top: Golgotha rock outcrop in Church of the Holy Sepulchre, Jerusalem.
Bottom: Traditional site of Golgotha.

54 Petra
(Rock)

The beautiful ruins of Petra, discovered in the early 1800s, are nearly hidden among the mountains of southwestern Jordan, in what was once West Edom, approximately sixty miles south of the Dead Sea. This ancient city's buildings were carved into the pinkish-red sandstone cliffs that are common to the area, giving Petra the nickname "Rose City."

People from all over the world visit the ancient city to see the ruins of temples, houses, a Roman basilica, a large amphitheater, and more than 800 tombs. The city was built in a valley known as the Wadi Mūsā (Valley of Moses). Legend says this valley is one of the places where Moses struck a rock in order to get water for the Israelites to drink (Exodus 17). Petra is also less than a mile from Mount Hor, where Aaron, Moses's brother, died (Numbers 20).

Some historians suggest that the city of Sela mentioned in 2 Kings 14:7 and Isaiah 16:1 is what we know today as Petra. Both *Sela* (Hebrew) and *Petra* (Greek) mean "rock." According to the biblical text, Sela, located in territory of the Edomites, was conquered by the Israelite king Amaziah.

Although the name *Petra* is not found in the Bible, archaeology has shown that the area where the ruins of Petra are located was inhabited by the Edomites around 1200 BC and that Petra was a vibrant city during the first century AD. Archaeological records also reveal the existence of a fourth-century Christian community in Petra. ■

Above: *Moses Striking the Rock* (1630), Pieter de Grebber (1600–1652).

Moses took the staff from before the Lᴏʀᴅ, as he commanded him. Then Moses and Aaron gathered the assembly together before the rock, and he said to them, "Hear now, you rebels: shall we bring water for you out of this rock?" And Moses lifted up his hand and struck the rock with his staff twice, and water came out abundantly, and the congregation drank, and their livestock.

NUMBERS 20:9–11

Above: Petra, Jordan.

CHAPTER NINE

Where Miracles Happen

The Bible is filled with events that are unprecedented in human history—events, some argue, that can only be explained as miracles. The *who*, *what*, *when*, and *why* of these occurrences are familiar to many Bible readers. Less familiar is the *where*. In the pages that follow, we'll explore the sites where some of the best-known and least-understood events in the Bible occurred:

- Rephidim
- Taberah
- Kadesh
- Pethor
- Gibeon
- En-hakkore
- Ashdod
- Beth Shemesh
- Mizpah
- Mount Carmel
- Gilgal
- Dothan
- The Decapolis
- Gadara
- Cana
- Gennesaret
- Mount of Olives
- Lydda
- Paphos
- Malta

Left: Gethsemane, olive orchard located at the foot of the Mount of Olives, Jerusalem, Israel.

55 Rephidim

The Israelites' journey through the Wilderness of Sin brought them to Rephidim, a ravine in southern Sinai that saw water only during the rainy season. Rephidim was bone-dry when the Israelites arrived, an alarming circumstance for a nation of people making their way across a desert wilderness.

The people turned to Moses in desperation. Frustrated by their short memories of how God had provided for them in the past, Moses sought direction from God, who told Moses to strike a particular rock with his staff. According to the biblical text, when he did, water flowed from the stone and the Israelites drank their fill.

The water from the rock was not the only marvel the Israelites witnessed at Rephidim. While camped in the ravine, they were attacked by Amalekite forces. Joshua assembled the Israelite army and led them into battle while Moses took up position on the hillside.

As he surveyed the battle below him, Moses made an unusual observation. Every time he raised his arms while holding his staff, the Israelite forces gained the upper hand in battle; when he lowered his arms, the Amalekites gained the upper hand. So Moses sat with his arms raised for hours, until the Israelites were victorious.

The location of this battle is often associated with modern-day Wadi Feiran, which is located near Jebel Musa (a mountain traditionally identified as the biblical Mount Sinai). The site is an oasis, a water source in a region with few of them, which would explain why the Amalekites were willing to battle for it. ■

56 Taberah

The Exodus from Egypt was undoubtedly a journey of faith. On their way to the land promised to Abraham and his descendants, the people of Israel traversed some of the least hospitable regions on the planet. The Bible narrative proceeds from the perspective that God had demonstrated his protection of and provision for the Israelites and had more than earned their trust.

That's why their frequent panic attacks and whining fits over their circumstances are portrayed as an affront to God. The great leader Moses was often reduced to the role of harried customer-complaint manager. Yet God demonstrated remarkable patience with the perpetually dissatisfied Israelites.

Occasionally, though, their grumbling reached a critical level and God took action. Such an event occurred shortly after the people left Sinai. As the Israelites complained about their hardships, God sent fire from heaven that burned the outskirts of their camp; as a result, a portion of the people died.

Thereafter, the site was known as Taberah, which means "burning." The location of Taberah has divided scholars for centuries. The Torah describes its location as three days' journey from Mount Sinai, which has led some scholars to identify it with modern-day Wadi Murrah, some thirty miles northeast of the southern tip of the Sinai Peninsula. ■

Above: Mountains in the Sinai desert, Sinai Peninsula, Egypt.
Right: Moses, Michelangelo (1475–1564), Church of San Pietro, Rome.

57 Kadesh

In order to properly understand the incident that occurred at Kadesh, it's necessary to review the events of Exodus 17:1–7. The Israelites had arrived at Rephidim during the dry season, found no water to drink, and began to panic. Water flowed from a rock after God instructed Moses to strike it with his staff, and the Israelites' thirst was quenched.

The same set of circumstances presented themselves at Kadesh, a region in the Wilderness of Sin (about 165 miles from Horeb) that formed the southern border of Canaan and the eastern border of Edom. The one difference between the two incidents is that, according to the Bible, in Kadesh God told Moses to *speak* to a rock. Instead, Moses repeated his actions from Rephidim and struck the rock (twice) with his staff. The Numbers narrative suggests that his frustration with the Israelites caused his lapse in following directions.

Water flowed from the rock, as it had in Rephidim, but the consequences of Moses's act of disobedience were severe. He and his brother, Aaron, who was also present, were forbidden from entering the land promised to Abraham and his descendants.

Kadesh is doubly notorious in Jewish history because it's also the place where the Israelites initially balked at invading Canaan for being intimidated by its inhabitants. As a result of their lack of trust, they were forced to wander in the wilderness for forty years. ■

 On Location

Wilderness Wandering

Moses commissioned twelve Israelite leaders to spy out Canaan, the land God had promised to Israel. When the spies returned, they reported that the inhabitants of the fertile land were "strong" and "of great height" (Numbers 13:27–28, 32). As as result, most of the Israelites complained to Moses and were afraid to enter the land.

Angry with the people for their lack of trust in him, God consigned them to forty years of wandering in the wilderness. None of the Israelites twenty years old or older who complained about entering Canaan would live to enter the land (Numbers 14:28–35).

58 Pethor

Pethor was the hometown of the prophet Balaam, who shows up in the Bible narrative near the end of the Israelites' forty-year sojourn in the wilderness. The nation's inexorable march toward Canaan terrified the people who stood in their way—namely, the Moabites and Midianites. Sihon, the king of the Amorites, had already fallen to the wilderness wanderers, as had Og, the king of Bashan.

Balak, the king of Moab, sent envoys to Pethor to enlist the aid of Balaam in the campaign against Israel. Balak wanted Balaam to pronounce a curse on Israel. According to the biblical text, Balaam consulted God, who warned him not to leave with the Moabite representatives. When Balak increased his offer, Balaam agreed to meet with him.

This angered God, who sent a sword-wielding angel to prevent Balaam's journey. Balaam couldn't see the angel, but his donkey could. Three times the beast of burden saved Balaam's life by changing course, stopping, or lying down in the middle of the road. And three times Balaam beat the animal for its obstinacy.

To get Balaam's attention, God gave his donkey the ability to speak and opened Balaam's eyes to the angel standing in front of him. Balaam quickly repented. God allowed him to continue his journey but warned him to say only what God allowed him to say.

So in the presence of the king of Moab, Balaam three times blessed the approaching Israelites. This infuriated the Moabite king, but it confirmed the inevitable: the Israelites would possess the land of Canaan.

Located west of the Euphrates on the modern Sajur River, Pethor, the place where a donkey spoke, is identified today with modern-day Tell Ahmar. ■

Above: *The Angel Appearing to Balaam,* Gustave Doré (1832–1883). **75**

59 Gibeon

The Israelites would not be denied the land of Canaan, which God promised to Abraham and his descendants. Some people—the Gibeonites, for example—made peace with that reality and established alliances with the conquering horde. Gibeon was a Canaanite city located about eight miles northwest of Jerusalem, along the route to Joppa.

Other nations chose to fight the inevitable to the bitter end. When Adoni-Zedek, the king of Jerusalem, learned about Gibeon's pact with Israel, he became alarmed. Gibeon was a valuable ally, full of well-trained warriors. Adoni-Zedek appealed to the Amorite kings of Hebron, Jarmuth, Lachish, and Eglon to join Jerusalem in an alliance against the Gibeonites.

The five kings launched a joint assault on Gibeon. The Gibeonites dispatched messengers to the Israelite camp at Gilgal, begging for help. The Israelite army responded immediately. Led by Joshua, they marched all night from Gilgal to Gibeon, taking the attackers by surprise.

Israel routed the invading forces. According to Joshua 10:11, those who tried to flee the battle were killed by giant hailstones, hurled by God. When it looked

as though sundown would interrupt the battle, Joshua commanded the sun to stand still. And it purportedly did—for an entire day.

Joshua 10:14 offers an apt summary of the extraordinary battle at Gibeon: "There has been no day like it before or since, when the LORD heeded the voice of a man, for the LORD fought for Israel."

Gibeon later became a center of worship during King Solomon's reign. The ruins of the ancient city can be seen near the modern-day Palestinian village of Al Jib. ∎

Top: Gibeon from Nebi Samwil.
Above: *Joshua Commanding the Sun to Stand Still upon Gibeon* (1816), John Martin (1789–1854).

60 En-hakkore

Samson was the scourge of Philistia.
Blessed with superhuman strength, the Israelite judge waged a one-man war against the Philistines. Ironically, his hatred of (almost) all things Philistine was matched only by his love for certain Philistine women.

When Samson's betrothed Philistine wife was given by her father to another man in marriage, Samson retaliated by burning Philistine grain fields, vineyards, and olive groves. The Philistines raised the stakes by burning to death Samson's intended bride, along with her father.

That set the stage for one of the bloodiest and most lopsided battles in the Bible. After launching several guerilla attacks on the Philistines, Samson retreated to a cave. The Philistine army set up position outside Samson's homeland of Judah and demanded that he be turned over to them.

> *With a donkey's jawbone*
> *I have made donkeys of them.*
> *With a donkey's jawbone*
> *I have killed a thousand men.*
> **JUDGES 15:16, NIV**

Then 3,000 frightened men from Judah confronted Samson in his cave and convinced him to let them tie him up and hand him over to the Philistines at Lehi.

Before the delivery could take place, however, Samson broke his restraints, grabbed a nearby jawbone of a donkey, and launched himself into the Philistine mob that had come to get him. By the time the beating was done, 1,000 Philistines lay dead at Samson's feet. The place became known as Ramath Lehi, which literally means "jawbone hill." Some scholars identify this location with the modern-day Wadi es-Sarar, near Zorah and Timnath.

When there were no more enemies to slay, an exhausted and extremely thirsty Samson cried out to God, who "split open the hollow place that is at Lehi, and water came out from it" (Judges 15:19). After drinking the water, Samson regained his strength.

Thereafter, the site was called En-hakkore, which means "the spring of him who called." ■

Zorah and the Sorek Valley from the south. Zorah is near Wadi es-Sarar

61 Ashdod

The ark of the covenant represented God's presence among the Israelites. As such, it was the holiest relic in all of Israel. When God allowed the Philistines to capture it, he was sending an unmistakable message to the Israelites about the importance of his presence among them.

Within Israel, the ark of the covenant was the source of incredible blessing. Outside Israel, however, the ark caused unimaginable devastation. The Philistines transported it to Ashdod, a city on the Mediterranean coast. (Today Ashdod is Israel's largest port and sixth-largest city. Tel Aviv lies twenty miles to its north, and Ashkelon lies twelve miles south.)

The temple of the Philistine god Dagon must have seemed like a logical place to hide the ark in Ashdod. However, when the Philistines came to check on it the next morning, they found the statue of Dagon fallen on its face on the ground before the ark.

Signs don't come much clearer than that, but the Philistines didn't get the message. They put their idol back in its place and left. The next morning, it was facedown on the ground again, but this time with its head and hands broken off.

According to 1 Samuel 5:6, God inflicted tumors on the inhabitants of Ashdod, who panicked and demanded that the Philistine rulers remove the ark from their city. The rulers moved the ark to Gath, and then to Ekron, but God's judgment continued—the residents of Gath suffered from sometimes fatal tumors. The devastation that occurred in clear connection with the ark of the covenant sent fear throughout the Philistine nation. ■

 On Location

The Lost Ark

During their forty years wandering in the wilderness, the Israelites carried the ark of the covenant along with them. According to Hebrews 9:4, the ark contained the two stone tablets on which were inscribed the Ten Commandments, as well as Aaron's staff and a jar of manna. Centuries later, when King Solomon built his temple, the ark was placed in the holy of holies, which only the high priest was permitted to enter once each year. In AD 586, after Jerusalem was conquered by the Babylonians, the ark was lost to history. Theories abound as to what happened to this preeminent religious relic for the ancient Judeans. Some suggest the ark was hidden under the Temple Mount or near Qumran by the Dead Sea. According to other theories, the ark was transported to various locations in Europe—or to Africa, where the Ethiopian Orthodox Church claims to be safeguarding it. A final possibility is found in 2 Maccabees, which describes how the prophet Jeremiah hid the ark in a cave on Mount Nebo in Jordan, where it will remain hidden until "God gathers his people together again and shows his mercy" (2:7 NRSV).

Above Left: Ashdod ruins.
Above Right: Illustrated re-creation of the ark of the covenant.

62 Beth Shemesh

After the devastation that followed in the wake of the Philistines' ill-advised capture of the ark of the covenant, the desperate captors were forced to return the ark to Israel. The Philistine rulers consulted their priests and diviners to figure out the best way to accomplish the task.

They devised a plan to load the ark, along with a gift of gold objects, onto a cart pulled by two cows and send it on its way, unaccompanied. If the cows took the path toward Beth Shemesh, the Philistines would know that the God of Israel was responsible for the devastation they had suffered. If the cows went anywhere else, they would chalk up the events to coincidence.

The cows headed straight to Beth Shemesh. It was a city in the territory allotted to Judah that sat on the border of the territory allotted to Dan. Beth Shemesh means "house of the sun," a reference to the ancient Canaanite sun goddess Shemesh.

The people of the city were harvesting wheat when the cart came to rest by a large rock nearby. They were overjoyed to see the ark of the covenant again. They stopped what they were doing, chopped up the cart for wood, and sacrificed the cows as burnt offerings to God. Their joy was tempered, however, when seventy people allowed their curiosity to get the better of them and looked into the ark. They were struck dead immediately.

Like the Philistines in Ashdod, the people of Beth Shemesh realized that their city was no place for the ark and made arrangements to have it carried away.

The ruins of Beth Shemesh are located in modern-day Tell er-Rumeileh. Modern-day Beth Shemesh boasts a population of around 110,000 people. ∎

Above: Beth Shemesh ariel view from northeast.
Above Right: Illustration of the ark of the covenant being sent away by the Philistines to Israel.

63 Mizpah

The city of Mizpah in the tribal territory of Benjamin served as a meeting place for the Israelites during times of national emergency. Its name means "watchtower," which refers to its location on the tallest hill in the region, some 600 feet above the plain of Gibeon. The city's proximity to Jerusalem (some four miles northwest of the capital city) made it accessible to many Israelites. Many scholars believe Mizpah and Nob (1 Samuel 21:1) refer to the same city. Today the village on the site is known as Nebi Samwil.

With the return of the ark of the covenant to Israel after its ill-fated capture by the Philistines, the prophet Samuel called the Israelites to renew their commitment to God. He urged them to get rid of their idols and their shrines to foreign gods. He called an assembly at Mizpah in order to sacrifice a burnt offering to God on behalf of the nation.

When the Philistines learned of the assembly, they saw an opportunity to catch the Israelites off guard. Their strategy was sound. The Israelites at Mizpah panicked

> Then Samuel said, "Gather all Israel at Mizpah, and I will pray to the Lord for you." Now when the Philistines heard that the people of Israel had gathered at Mizpah, the lords of the Philistines went up against Israel. And when the people of Israel heard of it, they were afraid of the Philistines. And the people of Israel said to Samuel, "Do not cease to cry out to the Lord our God for us, that he may save us from the hand of the Philistines." So Samuel took a nursing lamb and offered it as a whole burnt offering to the Lord. And Samuel cried out to the Lord for Israel, and the Lord answered him.
>
> 1 SAMUEL 7:5, 7–9

when they saw the Philistine forces approaching. Samuel, on the other hand, prayed for God to get involved.

According to 1 Samuel 7, Samuel's prayer was answered with earthshaking thunder from heaven—a sound so terrifying that it threw the charging Philistines into a panic. The Israelites regained their composure and ran after their suddenly retreating enemies. Because of the thunderous intervention at Mizpah, the Israelites managed to rout their Philistine enemies. ∎

Mizpah (Nebi Samwil) excavations.

64 Mount Carmel

King Ahab and his queen, Jezebel, were perhaps the most evil monarchs ever to reign in Israel. The idolatrous couple encouraged Baal worship throughout Israel. They installed 850 prophets of Baal and Asherah in their royal government, even as they tried to wipe out the remnant of God's prophets in the land.

Elijah wasn't afraid. The venerable prophet confronted King Ahab face-to-face and proposed a winner-take-all challenge. On one side would be 450 prophets of Baal. On the other side would be him, Elijah, alone—the sole representative of the God of Israel.

The site was Mount Carmel in northern Israel. The rules were simple: Each side would build an altar and prepare a sacrifice for its god. The deity who responded by sending fire to consume its sacrifice would be declared the true God of Israel.

The prophets of Baal went first. They prepared their altar and sacrifice and prayed for their god to accept it. When that didn't work, they danced wildly around the altar and even cut themselves to arouse Baal's attention.

They begged and pleaded from morning until evening, but to no avail. Their sacrifice remained untouched.

The people of Israel were watching, and Elijah wanted there to be no doubt about what was about to happen—or who was responsible. When Elijah's turn came, he built an altar of stones, dug a trench around it, and prepared a sacrifice on top of it. He then asked bystanders to fill four jugs with water and pour the water over his sacrifice. They filled the jugs and poured the water three times until everything was drenched and the trench was filled with water.

Elijah prayed and asked God to answer him. According to 1 Kings 18:38, a fire rushed from heaven and consumed his sacrifice, his stone altar, the water in the trench, and the soil around it. On Mount Carmel, God demonstrated that he alone was God of Israel.

The name *Mount Carmel* refers to a mountain range that extends from the Mediterranean coast toward the southeast. Several towns—including Haifa—are located on the slopes of Mount Carmel. ■

Above: View of the Jezreel Valley from Mount Carmel.　Middle: Jezebel seals.

65 Gilgal

Gilgal, a city most likely tucked away in the hill country of Ephraim, holds significance in being the first place where the people of Israel camped after crossing the Jordan River into Canaan (Joshua 4:19–20).

The prophet Samuel made frequent visits to Gilgal in order to offer sacrifices (1 Samuel 7:16, 10:8). Saul, the first king of Israel, was proclaimed king in Gilgal before the people of Israel (1 Samuel 11:14–15).

Gilgal was home to a school of the prophets. Chief among them was Elisha, who had served as an apprentice to the great prophet Elijah. According to 2 Kings 4, the region was in the midst of a devastating drought. That would explain why Elisha's servant had to scavenge the surrounding fields for herbs and wild vines to use for a stew to feed the prophets.

As the stew was served, however, the prophets noticed something was amiss. A poisonous plant had been added to the pot. Elisha acted quickly. He threw flour into the pot, which miraculously counteracted the poison.

The modern-day village of Jaljulia, located about four miles from both Bethel and Shiloh, could be the site of this near-fatal meal. ■

66 Dothan

The city of Dothan lay on the caravan route from Syria to Egypt, about twelve miles north of Samaria. According to Genesis 37:17, Joseph's brothers used that route when they sold Joseph into slavery from Dothan.

The city is perhaps best known in the Bible as the dwelling place of the prophet Elisha during the time Israel was at war with Aram. Elisha angered the king of Aram by warning the king of Israel to avoid certain places where Aramean forces were lying in wait for him.

The Arameans discovered where the pesky prophet lived and surrounded Dothan with mounted soldiers and chariots. Elisha's servant panicked when he saw the vast number of enemy soldiers, but Elisha stayed calm. He could see what his servant couldn't (until God opened his servant's eyes): hills filled with the invisible army of God, ready to protect Elisha.

As the Aramean army advanced on Elisha, he prayed for the soldiers to be struck blind. According to 2 Kings 6:18, God honored his request. Elisha then explained to the frightened, sightless soldiers that they had come to the wrong city. He led them to Samaria, where the king of Israel and his army were located. Instead of killing his enemies, the king gave them a feast and sent them home. From that day on, Aram ended its raids on Israel.

Today the site where the Aramean army was struck blind is known as Tell Dothan and can be found on the south side of the plain of Jezreel, in the hills of Gilboa. ■

Top Left: Tomb of the prophet Samuel.
Left: Tell Dothan, with ruins.   Above: Dothan tomb jug.

67 The Decapolis

The district of the Decapolis, which lay east of the Jordan River, featured ten primary cities (hence the name; *deca* means "ten" and *polis* means "city"). Though it was officially part of Israel, it was inhabited mostly by Gentiles, which gave it a foreign feel to many first-century Jewish people. The fact that herds of swine were kept in the district—in direct violation of the Law of Moses—may suggest that the people of the Decapolis had an antagonistic attitude toward their Jewish neighbors.

That may account for why the region plays such a small role in the New Testament narrative. Its most significant moment in the Bible spotlight occurs during Jesus's visit there after he passed through Tyre and Sidon. The people of the Decapolis brought to him a deaf and nearly mute man. Mark 7 describes how Jesus placed his fingers in the man's ears and on his tongue and said, "Ephphatha" ("Be opened"). The man was overjoyed to find that he could hear and speak clearly.

Ironically, the non-hearing-impaired people of the Decapolis turned a deaf ear to Jesus. After healing the man, Jesus instructed the man's companions not to tell anyone what had happened, apparently not wanting his healing ministry to overshadow his message. The man's shocked and amazed companions, however, proceeded to tell everyone they saw about Jesus's miraculous healing of their friend. They marveled, "He even makes the deaf hear and the mute speak" (Mark 7:37). ∎

> *And great crowds followed [Jesus] from Galilee and the Decapolis, and from Jerusalem and Judea, and from beyond the Jordan.*
> **MATTHEW 4:25**

Umm Qais in the ancient region of the Decapolis, present-day northern Jordan.

68 Gadara

Gadara, a fortified city of Decapolis, served as the capital of the Roman province of Perea. Positioned at the summit of a mountain about six miles southeast of the Sea of Galilee, Gadara was inhabited primarily by Gentiles. The land of the Gadarenes (or Gerasenes, as it appears in some Bible translations) extended to the Jordan River and the Sea of Galilee. Herds of pigs—animals that were forbidden in Israel—were not an unusual sight within its borders. The image of those roaming herds in a mountainous landscape sets the scene for the miracle recorded in Mark 5.

The first person Jesus encountered on his visit to the Gadarene territory was a demon-possessed madman who lived in the region's hillside tombs and terrorized passersby. The people of Gadara had tried to restrain him with chains and shackles, but the man was strong enough to break both.

The narrative of Mark's Gospel indicates that the man—or, rather, the demons inside him—recognized Jesus's superior power immediately. The man fell to his knees in front of Jesus and begged for mercy. The demons, knowing they were about to be exorcised, asked Jesus to send them into a nearby herd of pigs.

Jesus granted their request, and the pigs, which numbered about 2,000, rushed headlong down an embankment into the Sea of Galilee where they drowned. When the people of Gadara came to investigate, they found the former demoniac in his right mind, sitting calmly, and the people who witnessed the miracle trying to explain what had happened.

Instead of crowding around Jesus, begging to have their own infirmities healed (which often occurred after people witnessed one of Jesus's miracles), the inhabitants of Gadara begged him to leave. The freshly exorcised man tried to leave with Jesus, but Jesus urged him to return to his homeland so he could serve as a walking testament to what had happened.

The tombs mentioned in Mark's narrative are still a prominent feature of Gadara's ruins, which are found in modern-day Um-Keis. ■

> And when he saw Jesus from afar, he ran and fell down before him. And crying out with a loud voice, he said, "What have you to do with me, Jesus, Son of the Most High God? I adjure you by God, do not torment me." For he was saying to him, "Come out of the man, you unclean spirit!" And Jesus asked him, "What is your name?" He replied, "My name is Legion, for we are many." And he begged him earnestly not to send them out of the country. Now a great herd of pigs was feeding there on the hillside, and they begged him, saying, "Send us to the pigs; let us enter them." So he gave them permission. And the unclean spirits came out and entered the pigs; and the herd, numbering about two thousand, rushed down the steep bank into the sea and drowned in the sea.
>
> MARK 5:6–13

Above: Gadara underground mausoleum.

69 Cana

In a culture where hospitality was paramount and one faux pas could ruin a person's social standing for life, a newly married couple in Cana faced potential disaster. They had allowed the unthinkable to happen: the wine had run out during their wedding celebration.

Their good fortune was to have in attendance that day a young rabbi who had not yet made himself known publicly. The rabbi's mother, who likely was a close friend of the groom's family, approached her son to see if he could help the couple.

The rabbi—Jesus—instructed a group of servants to fill six water jars to the brim with water. Each jar held twenty to thirty gallons. Jesus then told the servants to draw some liquid from one of the jars and offer it to the master of the banquet. The master tasted the liquid and then marveled about how the groom had defied tradition by saving his very best wine for last.

And so Cana, a nondescript village in Galilee situated on the slope of a hill, secured its place in Bible history as the site of Jesus's first recorded public miracle—turning water into wine. ■

70 Gennesaret

After Jesus's miracle of walking on water, he climbed into his disciples' boat for a more traditional crossing of the Sea of Galilee. The boat landed at Gennesaret, on the western shore. Also known as Kinnereth (or Chinnereth) in the Hebrew Bible, the city was situated on an important trade route, about halfway between Capernaum and Magdala. From its elevated position, it overlooked the fertile plain of Gennesaret, which was known as "the Paradise of Galilee." As the city rose in prominence, its name replaced "Galilee" as the moniker for the body of water it bordered. The Sea of Galilee became known as Lake Gennesaret.

The city's only noteworthy appearance in the Bible, however, concerns what happened after Jesus and his disciples made landfall there. Jesus's reputation apparently preceded him that day. People with all manner of sickness and disability greeted him, clamoring for just a touch of his garment. According to Matthew 14:36, "as many as touched it were made well." ■

Below left: Sea of Galilee, Israel.

71 Mount of Olives

The Mount of Olives, a two-mile-long flattened ridge that rises some 200 feet above the Kidron Valley, is one of the most recognizable features of Jerusalem's landscape. Located less than a mile east of the Temple Mount, the mountain serves as the backdrop for many Bible stories.

King David crossed the mountain to escape his son Absalom's rebellion. King Solomon built pagan altars there. Jesus delivered a sermon there sometimes called "the Olivet discourse." The Garden of Gethsemane, where Jesus spent his final hours before his arrest, is somewhere down the mountain. According to Acts 1, after his resurrection Jesus ascended to heaven from the top of the Mount of Olives.

When Jesus traveled from Bethany to Jerusalem, his route took him over the mountain. Matthew 21 tells of one such journey. Jesus awakened early one morning in Bethany to begin his trip to Jerusalem. He grew hungry along the way and stopped at a fig tree to pick some fruit.

But the fig tree bore only leaves. There was no fruit to be picked. Jesus said, "May no fruit ever come from you again!" (Matthew 21:19). Immediately the fig tree withered as Jesus's astonished disciples looked on. ∎

> In the morning, as he was returning to the city, he became hungry. And seeing a fig tree by the wayside, he went to it and found nothing on it but only leaves. And he said to it, "May no fruit ever come from you again!" And the fig tree withered at once.
>
> When the disciples saw it, they marveled, saying, "How did the fig tree wither at once?" And Jesus answered them, "Truly, I say to you, if you have faith and do not doubt, you will not only do what has been done to the fig tree, but even if you say to this mountain, 'Be taken up and thrown into the sea,' it will happen. And whatever you ask in prayer, you will receive, if you have faith."
>
> MATTHEW 21:18–22

Mount of Olives, Jerusalem, Israel,

72 Lydda

On the northern road from the port city of Joppa to the capital city of Jerusalem, the first town a first-century traveler would encounter was Lydda. Known in the Hebrew Bible as Lod and today as Ludd, the town sits on the plain of Sharon, in the ancient tribal land of Ephraim.

The town achieved a degree of historical notoriety as the burial site of George, the patron saint of England. The ruins of a church built on top of his remains still can be seen. In the Bible, however, the city is known primarily for a remarkable incident involving the apostle Peter.

The Peter described in Acts 9 is very different from the impetuous, fickle disciple described in the Gospels. Gone is the panicked coward who abandoned Jesus on the night of his arrest. In his place is an energized and emboldened champion of the Christian faith. Among the earliest leaders of the first-century church, Peter had one of the highest profiles. In his ministry, he traveled throughout the region, encouraging believers and evangelizing unbelievers.

During his visit to Lydda, Peter encountered Aeneas, a man who was paralyzed and had been confined to his bed for eight long years. Acts 9:34–35 picks up the story:

> And Peter said to him, "Aeneas, Jesus Christ heals you; rise and make your bed." And immediately he rose. And all the residents of Lydda and Sharon saw him, and they turned to the Lord.

Christians consider the miracle in Lydda one of the earliest signs that the work of Jesus would continue through his disciples. ∎

73 Paphos

Paphos served as the capital of the island of Cyprus in the eastern Mediterranean Sea. The name causes scholars some confusion, as there were two cities called Paphos on the island, approximately ten miles apart. One was Old Paphos, the ancient site of a famous temple to the goddess Aphrodite. (According to mythology, Paphos is where she rose from the sea foam.) The other—the capital—was New Paphos, a coastal city on the western end of the island. This is the city mentioned in the Acts of the Apostles. Today New Paphos is called Baffa.

During their first missionary journey, Paul and Barnabas visited Paphos, where they encountered a Jewish sorcerer and false prophet named Elymas (or Bar-Jesus). Elymas served as an attendant to Sergius Paulus, the Roman governor of the island, and enjoyed his status as a VIP.

When the governor showed an interest in Paul and Barnabas's teachings, Elymas must have sensed that his days among the political elite of Paphos were numbered. He argued vehemently against the missionaries, trying desperately to prevent his meal ticket from switching his religious affiliation.

Paul stopped him dead in his tracks with some pointed accusations: "You son of the devil, you enemy of all righteousness, full of all deceit and villainy" (Acts 13:10). The apostle warned that Elymas would be struck blind temporarily for opposing his message. As the suddenly sightless sorcerer stumbled about begging for someone to guide him, the Roman governor believed the teachings about God and converted to Christianity. ∎

74 Malta

Malta is a small, rocky island in the Mediterranean Sea, about sixty miles south of Sicily. The island's strategic location made it a major player in Mediterranean trade and naval concerns for thousands of years. Not surprisingly, possession of the island changed hands frequently. The Phoenicians lost it to the Greeks, who lost it to the Carthaginians, who lost it to the Romans.

Also known as Melita, the island was under Roman rule when the apostle Paul was shipwrecked there while being transported as a prisoner to Rome. Paul made a memorable first impression on the island natives. As he was gathering sticks for a fire, a viper bit his hand. The islanders saw justice in the attack—the prisoner had cheated death in the sea but would pay for it with certain death from the snake's venom. When Paul suffered no ill effects from the bite, the islanders decided he was a god instead of a criminal.

Paul's subsequent impressions on the people of Malta were memorable too. According to Acts 28:8, when he learned that the father of Malta's governor was seriously ill, Paul visited the man, prayed for him, placed his hands on him, and healed him. Understandably, that motivated every other sick person on the island to seek an audience with Paul. The apostle healed them, too. He stayed on the island for three months.

Today Malta, which covers approximately 120 square miles and boasts a population of some 450,000 people, is one of the smallest and most densely populated nations in the world. Its capital, Valletta, is the smallest capital city in the European Union. The uninhabited Saint Paul's Island, located in a small inlet on the north side of Malta, is traditionally known as the site of Paul's shipwreck. ∎

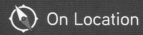
Shipwrecked on Malta

In Acts 27, the apostle Paul tells his harrowing story of being shipwrecked on the Mediterranean Sea while a prisoner on his way to trial in Rome. At first his journey was uneventful: "But soon a tempestuous wind, called the northeaster, struck down from the land. . . . When neither sun nor stars appeared for many days, and no small tempest lay on us, all hope of our being saved was at last abandoned" (verses 14, 20). Paul announced to the crew that an angel of God had appeared to him promising that there would be no loss of life: "So take heart, men, for I have faith in God that it will be exactly as I have been told. But we must run aground on some island" (verses 25–26). As the ship struck a reef and began to break up, the centurion ordered the crew and prisoners to make for land as best they could. As the angel promised, all survived: "After we were brought safely through, we then learned that the island was called Malta" (28:1).

Above right: *Shipwreck at Malta*, Gustave Doré (1832–1883).   Bottom: Valletta, Malta.

CHAPTER TEN

To the Ends of the Earth

Among *Jesus's last words to his followers* was a command to "make disciples of all nations" (Matthew 28:19–20). The emboldened disciples proved themselves to be more than equal to the task. In the face of unprecedented Roman persecution, these early missionaries carried the message to every corner of the known world. In the pages that follow, we'll explore some of the disciples' most noteworthy destinations, including the following:

- Arabia
- Caesarea
- Seleucia
- Salamis
- Perga
- Iconium
- Derbe
- Samothrace
- Philippi
- Amphipolis
- Thessalonica
- Berea
- Athens
- Corinth
- Ephesus
- Macedonia
- Rome
- India
- Ethiopia

Left: The Parthenon, temple on the Acropolis of Athens, Greece.

75 Arabia

The adult life and ministry of the apostle Paul is well documented in the Bible, mostly from the apostle's own writings. For many stops along the way, the Bible offers details as to who he encountered, what kind of reception he received, and how he interacted with the people there.

One notable exception is found in Galatians 1:17–18. In describing the events that followed his conversion, Paul said, "nor did I go up to Jerusalem to those who were apostles before me, but I went away into Arabia, and returned again to Damascus. Then after three years I went up to Jerusalem to visit Cephas and remained with him fifteen days."

In a few casually declarative sentences, Paul referenced a critical three-year span of his life that isn't mentioned anywhere else in the Bible.

The years are likely AD 34–37. The location is more difficult to pinpoint. The word *Arabia* may refer to the entire peninsula between the Red Sea and the Persian Gulf. Or it may refer to a smaller, more specific region—perhaps modern-day Lebanon.

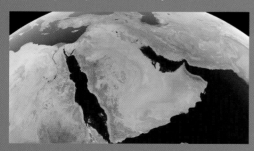

Did Paul travel far from Damascus? Did he embark on a pilgrimage to places associated with spiritual ancestors such as Moses and Elijah? How did he support himself for three years? How did he spend his time? These are just some of the tantalizing questions left unanswered by the Bible's reference to Paul's sojourn in Arabia. ∎

76 Caesarea

Caesarea was a coastal city on the Mediterranean Sea, located midway between modern-day Tel Aviv and Haifa. As was the case with many cities in the region, Caesarea changed hands—and names—several times. Under the Sidonians in the fourth century BC, it was known as Strato's Tower. The Hasmoneans captured it in 96 BC, followed by the Romans in 63 BC. Marc Antony offered the city as a gift to Cleopatra. Later it came under the control of Herod, who renamed it after Caesar.

As the capital of the Roman province of Judea, Caesarea functioned as headquarters for Roman troops in the region. The city also served as the backdrop for several New Testament stories. Perhaps most significantly, Caesarea was the home of Cornelius, the first Gentile to receive the message from the apostle Peter (Acts 10).

After an attempt was made on Paul's life in Jerusalem, his allies whisked him away to the safety of Caesarea, where he found passage to Tarsus (Acts 9:30). Paul returned to Caesarea on both his second and third missionary journeys. Later he was put on trial and held prisoner in the city for two years (Acts 23–24) before he appealed his case in Rome.

The city was home to Philip the evangelist and his four prophet daughters (Acts 21:8–9). Several ancient sources indicate that Herod Agrippa died there. After delivering a speech, the king was hailed as a god by the people of the city. According to Acts 12, when Herod refused to acknowledge God, he was struck dead in Caesarea. ∎

Above: Roman arches in Caesarea.

77 Seleucia

Seleucia, a seaport near the mouth of the Orontes River, was built by Seleucus I Nicator in the fourth century BC. Many other cities of that era could make the same claim of origin. Seleucus I Nicator, who served as a general for Alexander the Great before establishing the Seleucid Empire, was known for his passion for building cities. He constructed over thirty cities, most of which had variations of Seleucid, Antioch, or Laodicea in their names—after himself, his father (Antiochus), and his mother (supposedly named Laodice).

The Seleucia that figures most prominently in the New Testament served as the port for Antioch, which lay sixteen miles east-southeast. That would explain why

> So, being sent out by the Holy Spirit, they went down to Seleucia, and from there they sailed to Cyprus.
>
> ACTS 13:4

Paul and Barnabas used it as a launching point for their first missionary journey.

Today Seleucia is identified with the small village of el-Kalusi. Among the ruins of the ancient city are two sturdy piers, referred to by locals as "Paul" and "Barnabas." ■

The Missionary Journeys of the Apostle Paul

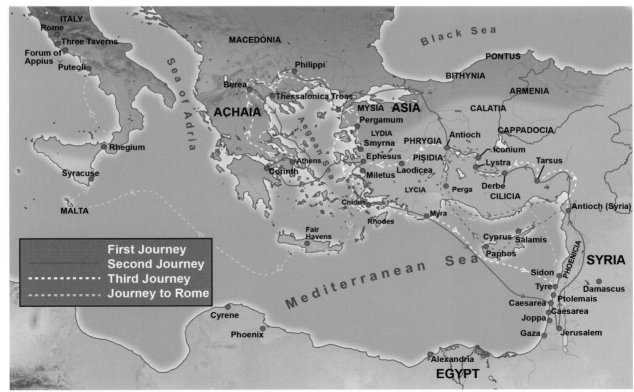

ITALY
Rome
Three Taverns
Forum of Appius
Puteoli
MACEDONIA
Philippi
Black Sea
PONTUS
BITHYNIA
ARMENIA
Sea of Adria
Berea
Thessalonica Troas
MYSIA ASIA
Pergamum
CALATIA
ACHAIA
LYDIA
Smyrna PHRYGIA
Antioch
CAPPADOCIA
Rhegium
Athens
Ephesus PISIDIA
Iconium
Tarsus
Syracuse
Corinth
Miletus
Laodicea
Lystra
Derbe
LYCIA Perga
CILICIA
MALTA
Cnidus
Rhodes
Myra
Antioch (Syria)
Fair Havens
Cyprus Salamis
Paphos
PHOENICIA
SYRIA
Sidon
Tyre
Damascus
Caesarea
Ptolemais
Cyrene
Caesarea
Joppa
Phoenix
Gaza Jerusalem
Alexandria
EGYPT
Mediterranean Sea
Aegean

First Journey
Second Journey
----------- **Third Journey**
----------- **Journey to Rome**

Above: A Roman sarcophagus on the hills of the ancient city of Seleucia. Photo courtesy of Htkava.

78 Salamis

Located at the mouth of the Pedieos River on the eastern shore of the island of Cyprus, the ancient city of Salamis welcomed maritime traffic from throughout the Middle East and Europe.

The straits off the shore of Salamis provided the backdrop for a historically significant naval battle between the Persian Empire and a group of Greek city-states in 480 BC. Through careful maneuvering and clever strategizing, the outmanned Greeks were able to score a decisive victory. Scholars point to that victory as a turning point in the Greco-Persian Wars. During the Roman era, Salamis was Cyprus's most important port and its most populous city.

In the New Testament, the city is noteworthy as the first stop on the first missionary journey of Paul and Barnabas (who was from Cyprus). According to Acts 13:5, the intrepid disciples "proclaimed the word of God" in the city's Jewish synagogues. The suggestion in Acts and other extrabiblical sources is that Salamis boasted a significant Jewish population. After making a name for themselves in Salamis, Paul and Barnabas—accompanied by Barnabas's cousin John Mark—traveled the length of the island on foot, preaching in city after city as they found opportunity.

The apocryphal book Acts of Barnabas identifies Salamis as the site of Barnabas's eventual martyrdom. Tradition holds that the "son of encouragement" (Acts 4:36) was killed by a mob of Jews organized by a man named Bar-Jesus. ■

First-Century Martyrs

Who	When	Where	How
Stephen	AD 36	Jerusalem	Stoned
James, son of Zebedee	AD 44	Judea	Executed by sword
Barnabas	AD 61	Salamis, Cyprus	Tortured and stoned [according to tradition]
James, brother of Jesus	AD 62 or 69	Jerusalem	Thrown down from the temple and stoned
Peter	AD 64	Rome	Crucified upside down [tradition]
Jude	AD 65	Beirut or Persia	Killed with an ax [tradition]
Paul	AD 67	Rome	Beheaded [tradition]
Mark	AD 68	Alexandria	Dragged through the streets [tradition]
Thomas	AD 72	India	Stabbed with a spear [tradition]
Philip	AD 80	Hierapolis	Crucified upside down [tradition]
Andrew	unknown	Patras	Crucified upside down [tradition]
Bartholomew	unknown	Armenia	Flayed alive and crucified upside down [tradition]
Matthew	unknown	Ethiopia	Sword [tradition]

Above: Saint Barnabas Church, Salamis.

79 Perga

The apostle Paul's first missionary journey took him and his traveling companions Barnabas and John Mark from the island of Cyprus north to Perga, a city near the southwestern coast of Anatolia (modern-day Turkey). The evangelists used Perga as a base from which they traveled to other cities in the region. Its primary appeal was a large Jewish population who welcomed the itinerant messengers.

As Alexander the Great had discovered nearly four centuries earlier when he occupied the city, traveling to and from Perga was a difficult task. Roman road-building projects had improved conditions considerably, but many scholars believe Paul and his companions' sojourns in the region frequently took them off the beaten path. Their desire to visit as many communities with Jewish populations as possible likely forced them to travel through some long and treacherous passes in remote locations throughout the region of Pamphylia.

Those conditions may help explain why John Mark abandoned his friends in Perga to return to Jerusalem. His fateful decision in the Pamphylian capital would eventually lead to the end of Paul and Barnabas's partnership.

In the fourth century, during the reign of the Roman emperor Constantine, Perga became an important Christian center and retained this status for the next two centuries.

The extensive ruins of Perga, located in the modern-day Turkish village of Murtana, have provided a wealth of information for students of the Roman world. ◼

> Now Paul and his companions set sail from Paphos and came to Perga in Pamphylia. And John left them and returned to Jerusalem.
>
> ACTS 13:13

Above: Ancient ruins of Perga.

80 Iconium

During his first missionary journey, the apostle Paul, along with his traveling companion Barnabas, introduced Christianity to the large and prosperous city of Iconium—probably around AD 45.

Acts 14 tells us Paul and Barnabas employed their usual strategy of taking their message to the local Jewish synagogue. In Iconium, that strategy produced decidedly mixed results. Verse 1 states that a great number of Jews and Greeks believed their message. Those who didn't, however, conspired to do harm to the evangelists. When their enemies' plot to stone Paul and Barnabas was uncovered, the missionaries were forced to flee the opulent capital of the Asia Minor province of Lycaonia.

Those enemies pursued Paul and Barnabas all the way to Lystra, where they convinced another crowd to stone Paul. Not one to let a near-death experience dissuade him, Paul likely returned to Iconium six years later during his third missionary journey to encourage and minister to the church that had been founded there.

Scholars associate Iconium with modern-day Konieh, a city in central Turkey that lies 120 miles north of the Mediterranean Sea, at the foot of the Taurus Mountains. ∎

Paul came also to Derbe and to Lystra. A disciple was there, named Timothy, the son of a Jewish woman who was a believer, but his father was a Greek.

ACTS 16:1

81 Derbe

The people of Lystra thought they had put an end to the apostle Paul's first missionary journey when they stoned him and dumped his body outside their city (see page 27). But the indomitable disciple surprised everyone by getting up, dusting himself off, and departing with his traveling companion Barnabas for their next destination: the city of Derbe.

Derbe was located in the extreme southeastern corner of the Lycaonian plain in the province of Galatia. Derbe was a frontier city of sorts, the last Roman territory on the road from southern Galatia to the east.

Little is known about Paul's experiences in Derbe. The fact that the New Testament makes no mention of persecution there suggests that his message was relatively well received. Among the converts in Derbe was a man named Gaius, who became a trusted ally of Paul's in the years that followed.

Scholars have yet to reach a consensus on the modern-day location of Derbe. Some identify it with a mound known as Kerti Huyuk in south-central Turkey, about fourteen miles north-northeast of Karaman. ∎

82 Samothrace

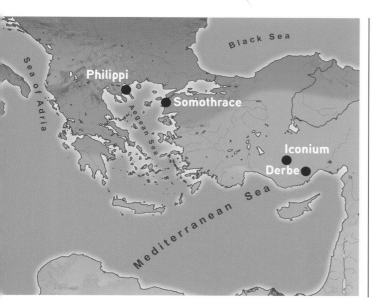

The island of Samothrace (or Samothracia) served two important purposes for first-century travelers sailing the Aegean Sea from Troas to Philippi. First, the island's mountainous terrain, which would have been visible on clear days for the entire journey, offered a continual reference point for those at the mercy of the waves and water. Second, its location at the midway point between Troas and Philippi made it a convenient stop for overnight docking.

That's how the apostle Paul came to the island during his first missionary journey. His ship, bound for Philippi, dropped anchor for the night in Samothrace. The Bible doesn't say how Paul spent his time on the island. But the fact that its inhabitants were known for their devotion to heathen cults and Roman mythology suggests that he might have engaged in a spirited debate or two.

Today the island is known as Samothraki. ∎

83 Philippi

Named after King Philip II of Macedonia, the father of Alexander the Great, the city of Philippi was a prosperous Roman colony strategically positioned along the Via Egnatia, one of the major trade routes of the ancient world.

Like the apostle Paul, many Philippians enjoyed the rights and privileges of their Roman citizenship. Bible scholars note that Paul appeals to the notion of citizenship as he discusses heaven in the letter he wrote to the church in Philippi (Philippians 3:20–21).

Many Philippians were retired Roman soldiers who had been granted property in the city in exchange for their service. Unlike most of the cities Paul visited on his missionary journeys, Philippi did not have a large Jewish community. There was no synagogue. At the Krenides River, Paul met a group of women with whom he shared his message. One of them, Lydia, a merchant who traded purple cloth, was baptized, along with her entire family.

She became a trusted and valued ally of the apostle Paul (Acts 16:11–15). Her conversion—and Paul's subsequent stay with her household—marked the beginning of the Philippian church.

Acts 16 describes one of Paul's most memorable incidents in Philippi. With his traveling companion Silas, Paul encountered a demon-possessed slave girl who had the power to tell the future. Paul drove the demon out of the girl, much to the dismay of her owners, who had gotten rich by exploiting her abilities.

The slave girl's owners hauled the two missionaries before the magistrates. Paul and Silas were stripped, beaten, flogged, and thrown into jail. Hours later, an earthquake shook the building, opening all the cell doors. Instead of escaping, Paul and Silas shared their message with the Philippian jailer, who converted, as did his entire family.

Scholars identify Philippi with the modern-day city of Kavala, Greece. Archaeological excavations of the ancient site have revealed Roman baths, basilicas, temples, Christian churches, and a fourth-century theater renovated by the Romans for gladiator contests. ∎

84 Amphipolis

As Paul traveled from Philippi to Thessalonica during his second missionary journey, he passed through a city built on a terraced hill at the bend of the Strymon River in northeastern Macedonia. The city, Amphipolis, had been founded by the Thracians in the fifth century BC as a military and commercial center.

At the time of Paul's brief visit, the city still boasted a thriving trade economy. Amphipolis produced (among other things) oil, timber, wine, figs, and woolen textiles. Its location figured heavily into its commercial viability. Amphipolis not only was situated along the heavily traveled Via Egnatia but also straddled the primary trade route from Thrace to Macedonia. Local gold and silver mines contributed to its wealth—and its desirability as a trading partner.

Archaeological excavations in the area of Amphipolis have yielded much information for scholars. The remains of a Roman aqueduct, a gymnasium, five churches, and various walls and bridges can be seen today. ■

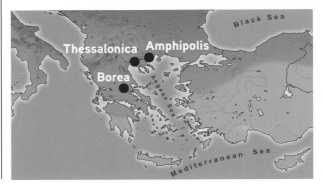

85 Thessalonica

Thessalonica became a key player in the ancient world because of its location. Situated along the Via Egnatia (the major overland trade route that ran from the Adriatic Sea to the Sea of Marmara), the seaport city on the Thermaic Gulf of the Aegean Sea also boasted a bustling maritime presence. With a population of over 200,000 people, Thessalonica was the largest city in Macedonia when the apostle Paul arrived there with Silas and Timothy during his second missionary journey, around AD 50. Paul undoubtedly recognized the city's strategic value as a spearhead for spreading his message throughout Macedonia and beyond.

On his first visit to Thessalonica, Paul preached at the synagogue on three different Sabbaths. His subject was prophecy—specifically, how the predictions of the Hebrew prophets had been fulfilled in Jesus. Yet not all of Paul's Thessalonian converts were Jews. According to Acts 17, a sizable percentage of the people who responded positively to Paul's message were proselytes, Greeks, and women of considerable social standing.

As Paul discovered time and again during his journeys, success breeds contempt. In Thessalonica, his Jewish opponents raised a mob to rid the city of the evangelists. When Paul and his companions couldn't be found, the mob turned their attention to Jason, the man with whom Paul and company were staying, as well as other converts. The mob dragged Jason and the other converts before the local magistrates and accused them of being loyal to a king other than Caesar. Though no evidence was found to convict Jason and the others, Paul and his companions recognized the danger they faced in Thessalonica and fled to Berea.

Paul returned to Thessalonica at least one other time in the years that followed. When he couldn't make it himself, he sent his fellow missionary Timothy to minister to the Thessalonian converts.

Paul wrote two epistles to the church in Thessalonica. Though it had humble beginnings, the church endured as a stronghold of Christianity for centuries.

The excavation of ancient Thessalonica is difficult because modern-day Thessaloniki, the second-largest city in Greece, was built on the site. However, many important discoveries are being made as the city continues to develop. ■

86 Berea

When a mob in Thessalonica threatened the life of the apostle Paul, his allies hustled him out of the city under cover of night. The group traveled west-southwest along the Via Egnatia for about twenty miles and then left the well-traveled roadway for a thirty-mile journey south. Their destination was Berea, a city in southwestern Macedonia.

The apostle and his traveling companions wasted no time sharing their message. They found a receptive audience in the city of Berea. A large number of Jews and Greeks—including many prominent citizens—believed. When the troublemakers of Thessalonica heard about Paul's ministry in Berea, they descended on the city to stir up crowds there.

Before they could do their worst, however, Paul was whisked away again, this time to Athens. He left behind the seeds that would produce a thriving church in the city—and two associates, Timothy and Silas, to help nurture it.

Today Berea is associated with Véoria, a small city located east of the Vérmio Mountains in northern Greece. ■

> The brothers immediately sent Paul and Silas away by night to Berea, and when they arrived they went into the Jewish synagogue. Now these Jews were more noble than those in Thessalonica; they received the word with all eagerness, examining the Scriptures daily to see if these things were so. Many of them therefore believed, with not a few Greek women of high standing as well as men.
>
> ACTS 17:10–12

Above: Hebrew handwritten Torah.

87 Athens

For a city that looms so large in ancient history, the renowned Greek center of philosophy, art, mathematics, athletics, and countless other disciplines maintains a decidedly low profile in the Bible. In fact, the only significant reference to Athens in its pages is found in Acts 17.

Having escaped an angry mob in Berea, the apostle Paul makes his way to the Greek capital with the help of some supporters. Distressed to find that the city is filled with idols, Paul initiates a one-man crusade to reason with the Athenians. He engages Jewish worshipers and God-fearing Greeks in the local synagogue, as well as merchants and shoppers in the marketplace.

Paul's teachings drew the attention of local philosophers, who brought him before the Areopagus, the Athenian supreme council, to present his beliefs. In the presence of such august company, the apostle delivered one of his most memorable defenses of the Christian faith.

The sticking point, as far as his Athenian audience was concerned, was the resurrection of the dead. While some embraced the concept and believed Paul, others sneered at the idea. With little response, Paul left Athens for Corinth. ∎

88 Corinth

The Greek city of Corinth was located on the isthmus that connects the Peloponnese to the mainland of Greece, about forty-eight miles west of Athens. The Corinth that the apostle Paul visited around AD 52 was a relatively new metropolis. The old city had been destroyed by the Romans in 146 BC and rebuilt a century later.

Populated by Romans, Greeks, and Jews, the city was renowned for its wealth as well as its immorality. The Temple of Aphrodite, where worship and prostitution were indistinguishable, set the moral tone for the city.

Paul stayed in Corinth for eighteen months on his initial visit. He supported himself by making and selling tents. It was during this first visit that he made the acquaintance of Aquila and Priscilla, a married couple (and fellow tentmakers) who became two of his closest

friends. According to Acts 20:3, Paul later returned to the city for a three-month stay.

Though many Corinthian Jews believed as a result of Paul's ministry, the church he established was made up primarily of Gentiles. To them he addressed the New Testament epistles now known as 1 and 2 Corinthians. ∎

Top Left: Herodion theater under the Acropolis, Athens, Greece.
Above: The ruins of the Temple of Apollo, Corinth, Greece.

89 Ephesus

As commercial and travel centers go, Ephesus had few equals in the ancient world. Located on the coast of the Aegean Sea at the mouth of the Cayster River, Ephesus boasted one of the busiest ports in the Roman Empire. Three major overland travel routes originated in the city. One led east to Babylon, by way of Laodicea; one led north through Smyrna; and one led south to the Meander Valley.

The architecture of the city contributed mightily to its cosmopolitan standing. One of the seven wonders of the ancient world, the Temple of Artemis (or Diana), was located in Ephesus, as well as the Commercial Agora marketplace, the Magnesian Gate, and the luxurious terrace houses that were built against Mount Coressus in the southern part of the city.

Acts 19–20 offers an overview of the apostle Paul's three-year ministry in Ephesus. As was his practice, Paul began his ministry in the synagogue. In Ephesus, though, he found an unreceptive audience among his fellow Jews. So he moved his base of operations to a lecture hall in Tyrannus. Every day for two years, the people of Ephesus could—and did—listen to Paul explain things to them "about the kingdom of God" (Acts 19:8).

According to Acts 19:11, "God was doing extraordinary miracles by the hands of Paul" in Ephesus. Handkerchiefs and aprons that he had touched were used to cure all manner of illness. He cast demons out of possessed people.

The number of Christians in Ephesus increased, a development that angered the craftsmen who made their living by providing trinkets for the pagan Temple of Artemis. They blamed Paul and his successful efforts for the reduced demand for their products and services. They raised a mob of like-minded Ephesians, seized some of Paul's traveling companions, and dragged them to the city's officials to make them answer for Paul's actions.

Paul wanted to go to the assembly, but his friends prohibited him. Eventually the crowd dispersed without incident and Paul departed Ephesus for Macedonia.

The church Paul left behind continued to grow in his absence, and it was to those followers that he addressed the New Testament epistle of Ephesians. ■

90 Macedonia

In the first century AD Macedonia was a Roman province that lay north of Greece. The district was bordered on the north by the Haemus (Balkan) Mountains, on the west by the Pindus Mountains, on the south by the Cambunian Hills, and on the east by a less-defined mountain range.

Alexander the Great ruled the kingdom of Macedonia from 336 to 323 BC and worked to expand his Greco-Macedonian culture—including Koine ("common") Greek—throughout the regions he conquered. The widespread adoption of the Greek language influenced its use in the writing of texts such as the New Testament. The Macedonian empire fell apart after Alexander's death, and the region eventually came under Roman rule.

The apostle Paul was summoned to the district in a vision by a "man of Macedonia" who begged Paul to help his people (Acts 16:9). Paul made immediate arrangements to sail from Troas to the Macedonian port of Neapolis. Shortly thereafter, the apostle witnessed the first conversions to Christianity by Europeans in Macedonia. ■

Top Right: Bronze relief depicting Alexander the Great and his army in battle.

(91 Rome

The specter of Rome looms large over the New Testament narrative. In the first century AD, Israel and the other nations that figure prominently in the story of Jesus and his disciples were part of the Roman Empire. The city of Rome was, of course, the seat of the empire. Scholars estimate that the population of the city at that time was about 1.2 million, half of whom were slaves. Opulence and overcrowding were the city's primary features.

Roman leaders were politically astute enough to grant a measure of autonomy to the nations under its control, especially in matters of religion. They stepped in only when they saw a potential threat to their ability to rule.

Case in point: Christianity.

When it was simply a Jewish rabbi and his twelve disciples, Rome did little to interfere. However, when those disciples began to recruit others to their cause, establishing pockets of followers called "churches" in regions throughout the empire—including Rome itself—the powers that be sensed a threat. And they moved quickly to stamp it out, using imprisonment, torture, and execution as deterrents.

The apostle Paul spent two years under house arrest in Rome. Many scholars note the likelihood that the epistles of Ephesians, Philippians, Colossians, and Philemon were written by Paul from Rome.

According to church tradition (and supported in part by 2 Timothy), Paul was executed in Rome by Emperor Nero around AD 67. Later tradition holds that the apostle Peter was crucified upside down in Rome around the same time. Countless other Christians were tortured and killed in Rome's Colosseum for sport and amusement. ■

> After three months we set sail in a ship that had wintered in the island, a ship of Alexandria, with the twin gods as a figurehead. Putting in at Syracuse, we stayed there for three days. And from there we made a circuit and arrived at Rhegium. And after one day a south wind sprang up, and on the second day we came to Puteoli. There we found brothers and were invited to stay with them for seven days. And so we came to Rome. And the brothers there, when they heard about us, came as far as the Forum of Appius and Three Taverns to meet us. On seeing them, Paul thanked God and took courage. And when we came into Rome, Paul was allowed to stay by himself, with the soldier who guarded him.
>
> ACTS 28:11–16

The Colosseum, also known as the Flavian Amphitheatre, Rome.

92 India

Jesus gives shape to his disciples' futures with a single sentence: "You will be my witnesses in Jerusalem and in all Judea and Samaria, and to the end of the earth" (Acts 1:8).

While many of his companions established ministries in Jerusalem and throughout Judea and Samaria, the apostle Thomas may have targeted the ends of the earth. Specifically, it is traditionally suggested that the former doubting disciple carried Jesus's message to the subcontinent of India.

Oral tradition passed down through generations in India tells of Thomas's travels to the southern tip of India in AD 52. His specific destination was the port city of Muziris (modern-day Pattanam) in the state of Kerala. If so, a Jewish community would have existed in Kerala at the time of his arrival. Lyrics to a seventeenth-century Indian song called "Thomma Parvam" ("Songs of Thomas") indicate that the apostle converted thirty Jews and 3,000 Hindus during his stay in Kerala. The *Didascalia*, a third-century text, states that a man named "Judas Thomas" led a

church in India. (The Greek historian Eusebius wrote that Thomas was also called Judas.)

The apostle may have eventually made his way to the southeastern city of Mylapore (near modern-day Chennai), where he allegedly ran afoul of the Hindu priests of Kali. Tradition suggests that Thomas was martyred either for insulting Kali or for converting its followers. December 21, AD 72, is the traditional date of his death.

Thomas's bones were supposedly buried in a church he founded in Mylapore. Some fifteen centuries later, Portuguese explorers built the San Thome Basilica on the spot. In 1893, the Bishop of Mylapore had it rebuilt. ∎

> *You will receive power when the Holy Spirit has come upon you, and you will be my witnesses in Jerusalem and in all Judea and Samaria, and to the end of the earth.*
> **ACTS 1:8**

93 Ethiopia

Tracking the movement of Jesus's followers after the New Testament narrative ends is difficult. Different sources offer conflicting accounts of their lives and ministries. The apostle Matthew, for example, is said to have been an evangelist in Judea before Roman persecution forced him to relocate his ministry to Parthia and Persia. Conflicting sources differ as to the location of Matthew's death.

According to Ethiopian Orthodox tradition (the most widely accepted tradition for Matthew's death), Matthew spent his final years in the African nation of Ethiopia on a mountaintop, praying and meditating. However, when an opportunity arose, Matthew responded, even when that meant baptizing the wife and son of an Ethiopian prince—against the wishes of the powerful prince.

The enraged royal ordered Matthew to be arrested and tortured. During the ordeal, Matthew died. His martyrdom in Ethiopia is celebrated on November 16. ∎

Top Right: *Martyrdom of St. Thomas*, Peter Paul Rubens (1577–1640).
Bottom: Pilgrims gather around the rock-hewn Church of Saint George in Lalibela, Ethiopia.

CHAPTER ELEVEN

Beyond the Book

Centuries *after the Bible's final words were written,* the book's seismic influence continued to reverberate in some of the most unlikely places on earth—largely due to the efforts of people who committed their lives to upholding the message of the Bible and communicating it to others around the world. As we wrap up our journey through astonishing cities, regions, and civilizations of the Bible, our attention shifts to six places that do not appear in the Bible's pages but rather attest to the scope of its influence:

- Nicaea
- Constantinople
- Timgad
- Hattusa
- Kaifeng
- Hispaniola

Left: Hagia Sophia, Istanbul, Turkey.

94 Nicaea

Christianity was still in its infancy when Constantine became emperor of Rome in AD 306. The new emperor ended Roman persecution of Jesus's followers. Yet internal divisions threatened to tear apart the fledgling religion before it could establish itself properly.

Chief among the divisions was the Arian controversy. A Christian leader named Arius taught that Jesus was created by God the Father and therefore not coeternal with the Father. His teachings were opposed by a vast number of other Christian leaders, including Athanasius, who affirmed that Jesus was not created but was fully divine and of the same eternal substance as God the Father.

Constantine recognized that religious stability and political stability went hand-in-hand, so he took an active role in trying to unify the quarreling factions of Christianity. The emperor invited hundreds of Christian leaders to attend the first worldwide church gathering, which began on June 19, AD 325. For the venue, he chose his lake house in Nicaea, a city in northwest Anatolia (modern-day Turkey).

At the Nicaean Council, church leaders backed Athanasius's teaching and constructed a profession of faith (which came to be known as the Nicene Creed) that is still used today. They also established a uniform schedule for observing Easter.

In AD 787, the Second Council of Nicaea was convened to restore the use of holy images in worship, a practice that had been outlawed for decades. ■

Above: Istanbul gate in ancient Byzantine city of Nicaea (Iznik).

Right: Icon depicting Emperor Constantine, accompanied by the bishops of the First Council of Nicaea (AD 325), holding the Niceno–Constantinopolitan Creed of AD 381.

NICENE CREED

I believe in one God, the Father Almighty, Maker of heaven and earth, and of all things visible and invisible.

And in one Lord Jesus Christ, the only-begotten Son of God, begotten of the Father before all worlds; God of God, Light of Light, very God of very God; begotten, not made, being of one substance with the Father, by whom all things were made.

Who, for us men for our salvation, came down from heaven, and was incarnate by the Holy Spirit of the virgin Mary, and was made man; and was crucified also for us under Pontius Pilate; He suffered and was buried; and the third day He rose again, according to the Scriptures; and ascended into heaven, and sits on the right hand of the Father; and He shall come again, with glory, to judge the quick and the dead; whose kingdom shall have no end.

And I believe in the Holy Ghost, the Lord and Giver of Life; who proceeds from the Father and the Son; who with the Father and the Son together is worshipped and glorified; who spoke by the prophets.

And I believe one holy catholic and apostolic Church. I acknowledge one baptism for the remission of sins; and I look for the resurrection of the dead, and the life of the world to come. Amen.

95
Constantinople

Two momentous events in history led to Constantinople's emergence as a religious and political center. The first was the decision of the Roman emperor Constantine in AD 330 to rename the city of Byzantium—the capital of the Eastern Roman Empire—Constantinople in honor of himself.

Constantine ended Roman persecution of Christians—and eventually professed Christianity himself. Appalled by the pagan influences that saturated Rome, Constantine wanted to create a capital that reflected his Christian sympathies.

The second event was the Great (or East-West) Schism of 1054 that divided the Catholic Church into Western Roman Catholicism and Eastern Greek Orthodoxy. Tensions between the four Eastern patriarchs of the church (Antioch, Alexandria, Jerusalem, and Constantinople) and the Western patriarch of Rome had been brewing for centuries. The root of the issue was papal authority. The four Eastern patriarchs balked at submitting to the Roman patriarch.

Add to that a complex host of other theological, linguistic, political, and geographical differences and you have the makings of an irreparable rift, with each side accusing the other of heresy. Christianity was forever altered by the split.

In the wake of the schism, Constantinople emerged as the center of the Eastern Orthodox religion, just as Rome was the center of its Western counterpart. Constantinople enjoyed a high profile on the world stage for centuries. Eventually the city was sacked by Christian forces during the Fourth Crusade (1202–1204) and later overrun by the Ottoman Turks (1453). ∎

Top: Ancient mosaic in Hagia Sophia in Istanbul, Turkey.
Middle: Gold coin of Roman emperor Constantine I, who ruled from AD 306–337.
Right: Depiction of the fall of Constantinople in 1453.

96 Timgad

Timgad was a key Roman city on the African continent in what is now Algeria. Its location near the main pass through the mountains gave Rome control of trade in the Sahara Desert region. The Roman emperor Trajan founded the city as a military colony around the end of the first century AD. Trajan offered veterans of the Parthian Wars land in Timgad in exchange for their continued military service. His goal was to keep the Berber forces of North Africa at bay.

His plan worked, and Timgad enjoyed peace for the first few centuries of its existence. In the middle of the third century AD a strong Christian presence began to assert itself in the city. In 397 AD, a church council was convened there.

Among the Christians who called Timgad home was a group of Donatists—followers of Jesus who took an extreme stance against those Christians who had renounced their faith in the face of Roman persecution. Because of their unforgiving stance and their radical teachings regarding sacraments (that is, they declared the sacraments invalid if given by people who had denied Jesus while suffering persecution from the Romans),

Donatists were labeled heretics by the Catholic Church. The Church urged Roman authorities to expel them from the city, which led to a standoff in 419 AD between the Roman government and followers of the Donatist bishop Gaudentius, who took refuge in Timgad's famed basilica and threatened to set it on fire if they were attacked. The standoff continued for quite some time; unfortunately, there is no record of how it ended.

Beyond its association with Christianity, Timgad stands as a classic example of Roman city planning. The sands of the Sahara, which swept over the site in the centuries after its abandonment in the eight century, proved to be an ideal preserving agent. Today the ruins of Timgad offer a glimpse of the grid plan of the city, as well as its theater, library, and basilica. ∎

Above: Ancient ruins of Timgad.
Right: Triumphal arch, called Trajan's Arch, Timgad, Algeria.

97 Hattusa

The Hittites are mentioned several times in the Hebrew Bible. Abraham bought a cave (in which to bury his wife Sarah) from a group of Hittites (Genesis 23). In Deuteronomy 20:17, the Hittites are listed among the nations that the Israelites must destroy in order to claim the land of Canaan. Second Samuel 23:39 identifies Uriah the Hittite as one of King David's "mighty men"—his most trusted band of soldiers. (David would later betray Uriah by sleeping with his wife, Bathsheba, and arranging for Uriah to be killed in battle.)

Hattusa, the ancient capital of the Hittite nation, goes unmentioned in the Bible. Little is known of its earliest history. The city was founded in the third millennium BC, and around 1700 BC, Anitta, the king of Kussara, conquered it and razed it completely. As a final insult, Anitta placed a curse on the ground on which the city was built—as well as on anyone who dared to rebuild there.

The Hittites tempted fate by constructing on the cursed ground an imperial capital, filled with impressive buildings, ornate temples, gates, and protective walls that ran for miles and contained hundreds of towers. Many of these features can still be seen among the ruins in modern-day Bogazkale, located in Turkey's Black Sea region.

Excavations at the site reveal that the city was destroyed again—this time burned to the ground—in the twelfth century BC. Scholars believe the inhabitants of Hattusa stripped the city of its valuables and its official records and then abandoned it sometime before the destruction took place. ■

Above: Ruins of Hattusa.

98 Kaifeng

Kaifeng served as the capital of the Northern Song Dynasty in China from AD 960–1127. More important than its political cache, however, was its location. Kaifeng was situated on a branch of the Silk Road—the fabled overland trade route that linked the East and the West. The Silk Road brought intrepid merchants from Europe, Africa, and other far-flung locations to China for the purpose of commerce.

Among the merchants who made the trip was a group of Jews from Persia or India. Instead of concluding their business and returning home with their goods, however, this group settled in China. Sometime during the time of the Northern Song Dynasty—and perhaps earlier, according to some scholars—these Jewish settlers established a community in Kaifeng. In 1163, their descendants built a synagogue in which to worship.

For centuries, the Kaifeng Jews practiced their religion, as they understood it, with no input from or contact with other Jewish sources. In the early 1600s, a chance encounter in Beijing between Ai Tian, a job-seeking native of Kaifeng, and Matteo Ricci, a Jesuit priest, brought the Kaifeng Jews to the attention of the outside world. When Tian learned that Ricci was a monotheist (worshiper of one God)—but not a Muslim—he concluded that Ricci must be a Jew, like himself. Ricci was stunned to discover the existence of a Jewish community in China.

The Jewish population apparently assimilated easily into Chinese culture. As the centuries passed, however, the community's knowledge of Jewish traditions diminished, and their faith became folklore. ■

Top Right: A group of street dancers in costumes, Kaifeng, China.
Above: Temple of the Chief Minister, Kaifeng, China.

99 Hispaniola

The expansionism—the quest to discover and claim new lands and new sea routes—that gripped Europe in the fifteenth and sixteenth centuries AD was fueled by economic and commercial necessities. The famed explorers of Spain, Portugal, England, and other European powers were looking for the most direct (and profitable) trade routes with the East.

Yet there was a secondary motive as well: religion. The Christian nations of Europe wanted to take the teachings of the Bible to the people of the New World. As early as 1510, religious orders started sending missionaries to the New World for the express purpose of evangelizing the natives. That's how the friars of the Dominican Order came to establish a presence on the island of Hispaniola (modern-day Haiti and the Dominican Republic).

Aware of the cruelty and exploitation that had been perpetrated by Europeans under the guise of converting pagans, the Dominican friars resolved to treat the people they would convert with dignity.

Inspired by their example, a young priest named Bartolomé de las Casas dedicated his life to bringing justice to the natives of the West Indies and Central America. He presented their case before the king of Spain. His efforts eventually led to the New Laws of 1542, which temporarily abolished the *encomienda*—the right of Spanish settlers to own a certain number of natives as slaves.

Because of his tireless efforts and widespread influence, Bartolomé de las Casas is now regarded by some historians as one of the pioneers of universal human rights. ■

On Location

The Mission Continues

In 1492, on his second journey to the New World, Christopher Columbus took five priests along with him. Two years later the first Christian missionaries arrived in what is now the Dominican Republic and Haiti. Over the centuries both Catholic and Protestant missions have evangelized these two countries. Currently, 95% of the Dominican Republic is Christian, and Haiti is 82% Christian.*

[Source: Central Intelligence Agency, The World Factbook, https://www.cia.gov/library/publications/the-world-factbook/fields/2122.html.]

Old village in the Dominican Republic (Altos de Chavón).

museum of the Bible

Experience the Book that Shapes History

Museum of the Bible is a 430,000-square-foot building located in the heart of Washington, D.C.—just steps from the National Mall and the U.S. Capitol. Displaying artifacts from several collections, the Museum explores the Bible's history, narrative and impact through high-tech exhibits, immersive settings, and interactive experiences. Upon entering, you pass through two massive, bronze gates resembling printing plates from Genesis 1. Beyond the gates, an incredible replica of an ancient artifact containing Psalm 19 hangs behind etched glass panels. Come be inspired by the imagination and innovation used to display thousands of years of biblical history.

Museum of the Bible aims to be the most technologically advanced museum in the world, starting with its unique Digital Guide that allows guests to personalize their museum experience with navigation, customized tours, supplemental visual and audio content, and more.

For more information and to plan your visit, go to museumoftheBible.org.